HEAL

An Owner's Manual for how to heal
emotional wounds and live your truth

AIMEE SEMAS-DAY, M.A., LMFT

 FriesenPress

One Printers Way
Altona, MB R0G 0B0
Canada

www.friesenpress.com

ISBN
978-1-03-913159-0 (Hardcover)
978-1-03-913158-3 (Paperback)
978-1-03-913160-6 (eBook)

1. SELF-HELP, EMOTIONS

Distributed to the trade by The Ingram Book Company

TABLE OF CONTENTS

Introduction	1
Chapter 1	
The Reptilian Brain	**5**
What is the reptilian brain?	6
What is the higher brain? How can it help us?	13
Humor	*14*
Exercises	16
Hopes and dreams	*17*
Exercises	18
The "I love" list	*20*
Exercises	21
Gratitude	*22*
Exercises	23
Looking forward	*24*
Exercises	24
Meditation	*24*
Random acts of kindness or service to others	*26*
Coping skills versus distractions	*27*
Exercises	29
Just three things	*30*
Exercises	33
Back to the reptilian brain	33
Exercises	34
A wrinkle to higher brain activation: the need to heal	38
Chapter 2	
Emotions, Repression, and Healing	**41**
Exercises	46
What happens when we can't release our emotions?	47
How do we release our emotional repressions?	50
Exercises	56

Chapter 3

Healing Trauma   **59**

How do we heal from trauma?   59

    Healing exercises   63

    Trauma visualization exercises   66

Triggers are messengers, and we can follow them to heal   73

    Trigger exercises   74

Emotions are messengers too   75

Chapter 4

Self-talk, the RB, and Repressed Emotions   **77**

Why do we listen to negative self-talk?   77

    Self-talk exercises   86

Chapter 5

The RB and Triggers in Romantic Relationships   **89**

Do romantic relationships hold the potential to help us heal?   89

What is the pursuer–distancer dynamic?   92

    Exercises   98

Chapter 6

Boundaries   **101**

What are healthy boundaries in relationships?   101

  Enmeshed boundaries   *103*

  Rigid boundaries   *107*

  What do flexible/healthy boundaries

  look like?   *108*

    Exercises   110

Chapter 7

Moving Forward—Goal Setting   **111**

    Exercises   112

Conclusion   115

About the Author   119

HEAL

INTRODUCTION

What if I were to tell you that you can truly heal? I mean truly heal, to the point where your scars and triggers no longer have the potency they once did and where you can show up being and expressing who you really are in any situation. What if you could live authentically—remaining connected to yourself in the moment while also connecting to others without feeling anxiety, depression, self-doubt, or alienation? And if negative feelings do crop up, as they do with all humans, you would know what to do about it.

This book is a vehicle that can bring you closer to living a life that is aligned with these ideals.

Together, we will explore the human condition on a neurological and emotional level so you can learn how to undo past traumas and heal mental health symptoms that may be limiting you from living a life that is true to who you are. Through understanding how to heal past scars, as well as discovering what happens in the brain when you experience challenging emotions, you can learn to develop strategies to overcome any obstacle— be it internal or external.

We will also learn how to interpret the messages your emotions and mental health symptoms are sending you.

Like a car's fuel light illuminates when it's low on gas, our symptoms and emotions are indicators telling us that there is something we need to do to be authentic, balanced, whole, and healthier. We just need to learn their language and learn what exactly we need to do. In this way, this book can also serve as an owner's manual that will help you understand yourself as an emotional being and ascertain what you can do to truly heal and ultimately feel more grounded, whole and connected to your truth.

Studies in neuroscience over the past two decades have revealed secrets of the human condition. In this book, we will explore some key discoveries that give us vital information for improving our mental health. These revelations include:

- why we respond to difficult life events the way we do
- why we experience lasting symptoms like depression, anxiety, rage, OCD, addiction, relationship conflict, and so on
- what is happening in the brain when all these experiences and symptoms are occurring
- and what we can do about it!

We will explore concepts including neural pathway processes in a very basic and accessible way so you can understand why you feel how you feel, why you perceive the world as you do, and why you choose the behaviors that you do. While bringing forth self-awareness and understanding, this information can lay the groundwork for you to make lasting changes—which is what this book is all about.

Once we explore the brain, we will delve into emotions and how they interact with the brain in response to difficult life events and how this all leads to symptoms that can be difficult at best, debilitating at worst. Emotions have always been an elusive animal within the human condition, one which many cultures dismiss as childish indulgences that need not be expressed. Unfortunately, this dismissive attitude has only perpetuated the inability to fully heal for many people. We will explore healthy ways of looking at emotions, and different strategies to allow our emotions to live within us, thereby learning how to process emotions so we can begin to heal from past traumas.

We will also delve into negative versus positive self-talk and how this ties back to our neuroanatomy and emotional climate, leaving you more equipped to know how to manage the chatter in your mind. This all culminates in the final chapters on relationships and boundaries, which will leave you with more clarity on how to have healthy interactions with others while remaining true to yourself.

To make this book less of me throwing lots of information at you and more of a collaboration, in each chapter you will find exercises that apply the topic of discussion. The way I formatted the chapters is by presenting information and then inviting the application of that information, making this book more of a workbook. Go at your own pace with the exercises. You might decide to read it all first and then go back and do them at your own speed, or you might also decide to focus on one chapter at a time and space out the other chapters. May this book be an explorative process that is unique to you. The hope is that it is both informative and interactive.

As was noted before, we will begin with a focus on developing good coping skills to aid you in feeling better, hopefully sooner than later, which will also provide tools to navigate the subsequent topics on emotions and healing past scars. An important disclaimer is that if you do require intense healing from past traumas and you haven't processed any of it yet, make sure to do deeper work with a licensed therapist. The exercises are really a supplement to previous or current treatment for traumas with high acuity. For everyone else who may have traumas or emotional scars that aren't as intense, you can follow along and complete the exercises as they feel comfortable for you.

Know that I'm here to give information that you get to try on so you can see how it fits with your life experience and how it may help you take your life to the next level of healing. I say *healing* because the "-ing" implies ongoing—it is a journey. Every new chapter in our life brings new insights that will heal another layer of the past, and therefore, I don't know if we ever truly arrive at a "healed" destination. I will say that the more we heal, the more grounded we are with the healing process and the more we are okay with it being something life-long. Because we embrace the learning and growth that comes with it, the pain that can come with healing lessens. From this place, we appreciate the truism that *pain inspires growth*, and I believe that is what we are all here to do, learn and grow.

There is a profound saying that encapsulates this idea, *"Once the storm is over, you won't remember how you made it through, how you managed to survive. You won't even be sure whether the storm is really over. But one thing is certain. When you come out of the storm, you won't be the same person who walked in. That's what the storm is all about"* (Haruki Murakami, *Kafka on the Shore*, 2002).

May your journey through this book change you in such a way that you leave feeling more you…and more connected to your truth. Hopefully, the information and techniques shared will give you the clarity, insight, and healing it has given me over the past two decades. In the end, this book really provides information we have all needed since the age of ten.

Enjoy!

CHAPTER 1
The Reptilian Brain

In the nineties, ground-breaking discoveries in neuroscience clarified, with detail, elements of the human emotional experience that were once elusive to description. These insights have helped to answer questions that were before unanswerable on a scientific level, like:

- What happens in the brain when we experience an emotional trigger?
- What happens neurologically to explain why someone can't change self-destructive behaviors or addictions?
- What happens when individuals can't seem to climb out of debilitating depression or terrifying anxiety?

Now, some of these questions have loosely been answered by psychologists in different ways throughout the past two centuries, but they have never garnered support completely from the scientific community. After all, we have never been able to really see the innerworkings of neuroanatomy before. Psychology was always seen as a soft science because it didn't provide anything tangible that could be observed or verified with one of the five senses. This is why the discoveries in neuroscience that show what is happening in the brain when we are experiencing difficult or intense emotions have crossed a threshold into a new world of understanding and hold mind-blowing ramifications for humanity. We can now understand and articulate our emotional experiences with scientific concepts and innerworkings.

What is the reptilian brain?

Let's explore how neuroscience has shaped a new understanding of how our brain works with our emotions in operationalizing difficult, as well as pleasurable, human experiences. We will start with gleaning a greater understanding of a structure in the brain known as the *reptilian brain (RB)*.

The reptilian brain, also referred to as the primitive brain, is a vital neurological structure whose very purpose is survival. This is the part of the brain we have in common with all animals, which is why it is considered primitive (it's been around as long as creatures have, likely because it holds the mechanisms that focus on staying alive). The function of the reptilian brain is to act when there is danger present. It really is a simple at that.

When activated, it only knows one of three responses: fight, flight, or freeze. So, if a lion were to walk into the room and look at you with hunger in its eyes, you would have three choices: freeze and hopefully blend into the background; courageously put up your fists and start boxing; or find the quickest escape route and run like hell. We have no other available responses when the RB is activated because all other parts of the brain are inaccessible. Further, when this part of the brain is activated, we aren't even thinking—we are doing, and we are physiologically called upon to do whatever the doing behavior is quickly. Thus, there is no time to pause or reflect, we must act immediately to attend to whatever is threatening our survival. When in use, other functions in the brain that provide responses like problem solving, big picture thinking, empathy/compassion, perspective, logic, assessing consequences, and hope are turned off. These are automatically dismantled when the RB is activated. And this makes sense going back to the lion in the room situation. Even though it would be nice if we could pause to access problem solving or logic, if we did, we would likely be eaten.

Time is of the essence when the RB is activated, so in the interest of expediency, we must act NOW and act QUICKLY. In turn, adaption selected the three F's as the best possible actions to enable survival in all situations that threaten our physical safety. Makes sense—super adaptive, right?

Now the wrinkle comes in with human beings. Unlike other creatures, this part of our brain doesn't just get incited when we are in physical danger. In fact, there are 2 other conditions that arise which put RB in the driver's seat:

#1 When we are emotionally activated or triggered
#2 When, due to a lot of use, we become stuck in our lower brain

In either situation when the RB is activated and there is no physical danger a problem arises because we find ourselves trapped with a brain that doesn't work properly. In these moments we have zero access to functions in the brain that might be helpful when in conflict or in day-to-day life, like problem solving, assessing consequences, logic, and perspective. These parts of the brain are inaccessible when the RB gets initiated, again in the interest of expediency and survival when RB is called upon everything else shuts down. So, when we are in our lower brain with no assailant to fight off, guess what happens next? Well, since there is no lion to be slayed or run-like-hell plan to be implemented, you are stuck with a brain that can't think correctly, because fundamentally this part of the brain is designed to act, not think. And since there is nothing to do outwardly in terms of the 3 f's, which would captivate your focus, you are stuck with your thoughts. Even if you are interacting with others, you will still be plagued with lower brain thinking; and since thinking is not what this part of the brain does, the thoughts that manifest are highly distorted, inaccurate, uncomfortable and take on a certain qualitative state such as:

- become highly muddled with no ability for clear thinking
- become black and white and all or nothing, which is because the RB thinks in terms of life or death, so it will use words like "always," "never," "nobody," "everybody," and so on
- become alarmed, panicked, and urgent ("everything" is an emergency and needs to happen now)
- lead you to distrust most people around (e.g., if you are fighting with you partner, they are suddenly your enemy, even though they were the love of your life five minutes ago)

- say to you "everything" is bad, it will "always" be bad, and it "always" was bad (overgeneralization of the current negative state)
- convince you that whatever you are thinking is 100% true and there can be no other way of perceiving the situation
- pull you into future-tripping by projecting your current fears onto the future with a sense of absolute certainty that it will unfold that way
- use fear constantly—whatever it tells you, the underlying emotional climate is always laced with FEAR and when you are in this part of the brain, fear is truly the only emotion you are experiencing, so any other emotion that might be there gets overlooked

As is evident from the list above we again arrive at the conclusion that the RB, when activated unnecessarily, creates a problem for the human experience. Let's look at an example of what this looks like in real life in the context of the first condition that puts the RB in the driver's seat: emotional activation or being triggered.

When we are triggered by something that happens in our environment, maybe someone says something, does something or we tell ourselves something we suddenly become activated emotionally and then our whole world turns upside down. What is happening neurologically when all of this is going on?

Enter the amygdala: the emotional part of the brain. For many of us, the moment we are triggered, and our emotions are ignited, the amygdala communicates with our RB, which automatically sends us into a tailspin. Suddenly we can't think straight and the 3 f's are enlisted unnecessarily. I say *unnecessarily* because if the issue is emotional in nature and not physical, you don't really need to be fighting, fleeing, or freezing, right? Again, if there is no physical danger present, then the taking over of the RB is not necessary and could cause more harm than good, just for the simple reason that the brain can't effectively communicate or problem solve when the RB is activated. When it's emotional in nature and not a threat to our physical survival we need the rest of our brain to navigate the situation successfully.

For example, let's apply this to a scenario where you are in conflict with a loved one and therefore triggered and in your lower brain. What happens here is that, from the place of distorted-RB thinking, your partner now becomes your enemy, and it is literally kill or be killed, even though moments before you were madly in love and everything was great. Now you feel as though your partner is a threat to your survival, so you defend yourself against the threat despite the relationship and despite the fact that there really is no physical danger. The ability to problem-solve dismantled, you become highly primitive in your communication with your loved one and the last thing focused on is the livelihood of the relationship. Everything is distorted and you are interpreting your partner's behaviors as a threat to your sense of self. Now, seeing this from the outside, it becomes obvious why being in RB while in conflict with anyone will not end well nor bode well for the health of the relationship. RB responses are not only ineffective but potentially damaging to our relationships when we are emotionally triggered. Again, RB is designed to act, not think and what emotional activation really needs is perspective, the ability to effectively communicate, see things clearly and regulate one's emotions—and the RB will 'never' be able to provide this. To make matters even more complicated, like mentioned above, when the lower brain is activated the RB thoughts will 'tell' you they are accurate. Like in the example above, you will believe that your partner is your enemy, and you must defend yourself.

The second condition where the RB takes over unnecessarily is when individuals are living in the RB all of the time without being triggered by anything in the moment. In this condition, there is no physical danger present or emotional activation but because the individual in question has used this part of the brain a lot it starts to rule and then they have the resulting experience of negative self-talk, fear, hopelessness and an overall feeling of gloom and doom. Because of this when folks live here all the time there is also going to be resulting mental health symptoms (which we will go into more detail later). All of this occurs because we lack access to the other parts of the brain that aid in big picture thinking, optimism and perspective. Further, going back to the RB lying to you- if you're living here all the time, the lower brain will also tell you that this is just the 'way life is' and that the gloom and doom feeling is just reality.

In all situations where RB is incited unnecessarily, whether we are emotionally activated or it's come to be our normal state of being, our RB thoughts will feel real, clear, and obvious. However, knowing that the RB is designed to act not think, and knowing RB thoughts are highly distorted, how accurate do you think these '*real, clear, and obvious*' lower brain thoughts are? To really drive home the point, it's important to note that when you are in this part of the brain, you are using maybe 2% of your brain—it's small, so I'll just use this number to get my point across. So, knowing this is, maybe, 2% of your brain and it is a part of the brain that is designed to act, not think, how accurate do you think the thoughts and perceptions that come from this part of the brain are? Not accurate at all!

We know reptilian brain thoughts are distortions and they are coming from a part of the brain not designed to think, it simply is not what this part of the brain does. So, thinking that we are getting a valid interpretation of reality from the RB is like believing your five-year-old can complete an algebra equation correctly. They might produce an answer, but it's likely not going to be right. Similarly, once we realize that the RB is not equipped to deal with emotional situations, we will learn not to take advice from this part of the brain, because the answer will almost always be wrong. And we will learn not to take our thoughts seriously when we are in this part of the brain either because we will know the RB does not perceive reality as it truly is.

Whether you experience reptilian brain dominance when you are triggered or maybe you are hanging out in that part of the brain all the time, we again arrive at the obvious conclusion, the reptilian brain should only be activated when physical danger is imminent. When we are in this part of the brain for any other reason our quality of life is greatly diminished and the bottom line is, when we live in RB we don't feel good.

With all of this in mind, the next questions are, how can we get out of this part of the brain and keep it from activating unnecessarily when we are emotionally triggered and/or how can we stop living from this part of the brain all together? The good news is *we can*; the bad news is how "easy" or quickly we can achieve these goals will depend a bit on our history with the activation of the RB. That is, if you have used this part of the brain a lot in your life or like we discussed previously if you tend to live here, it will take more work to keep it from taking over.

Let's explore this a little more deeply by looking at the 'bad' news which entails understanding why both traumas and triggers activate the lower brain.

If we have experienced a trauma at some point in our life, the RB will activate because traumas are a threat to our sense of self, whether there is overt physical danger present or not. And experiences like physical/sexual abuse, neglect, natural disasters, bullying, and so on are also physically threatening, so they will naturally all activate the RB. Emotional abuse also incites the lower brain, as was discussed before the amygdala frequently enlists the 3 f's because of the distress experienced. So any form of trauma, be it physical or emotional will ignite a RB response in the interest of survival. What was discovered with individuals who have had a history of trauma and therefore lower-brain activation, is the lower brain starts to develop neural pathways that become highly solidified in response to that activation. The brain, being a muscle, becomes strengthened in the areas it's used the most, and especially the most intensely. Once these neural pathways are established, they become ingrained and very difficult to undo. Individuals who have had a lot of trauma or significant trauma (by the way, all trauma is significant) could start to live in this part of the brain because the muscle has become strong and therefore dominant. In these cases, the neural pathways become ingrained, and the responses emitted during the trauma event(s) will become a generalized response.

If you shut down during the trauma, you will likely shut down in triggering situations after the trauma. Same goes if you were more of a fighter, you will likely find yourself on edge and/or aggressively posturing toward others when triggered. Our triggers are intimately linked to our past history and this is why emotional activation sets off the RB so easily. Anything that feels similar to the original trauma will come to trigger the lower brain just like it did when the trauma itself occurred. This is what a trigger truly is- a reverberation of the emotions tied to a trauma memory that's being incited in the moment because the circumstances are similar. Further, if you have had a number of traumas and/or the traumas were intense, this part of the brain will become so strong that you will likely come to live from this place all the time. Once you live in the lower brain consistently, you will eventually come to experience symptoms like anxiety, depression, rage, OCD, and have extreme or consistent triggers. All of these mental health symptoms tell you that you are in your lower brain, and if these symptoms are chronic, it simply means that you are in your lower brain all the time.

When we live in the lower brain, we will eventually need to medicate in some way or another to manage the intensity of the fear-based life experience, so addictions become a means of coping, self-soothing, and numbing the discomfort of being in lower brain. Addictions can be any form of distraction. This includes not only alcohol and other substances, but also food, social media, TV, video games, codependent relationships, gossiping and shopping, just to name a few.

Another piece of bad news is that once we live in the RB for a significant amount of time, this way of being becomes ingrained, unconscious, and highly resistant to change. In other words, we become utterly stuck— the RB thoughts are so distorted, fear based, and again convincing that we believe there is nothing wrong with how we are perceiving the world and experiencing life and, therefore, why would we try to change it?

The resistance to change could keep you imprisoned to the RB in a negative feedback loop, which looks something like this: you feel horrible and think in such a negative fashion that you create negative experiences out in the world that just reinforce why the RB thoughts that say that the world is threatening and unsafe are true. All of this naturally results in being impervious to change. And since we believe the RB thoughts are 100% true (even though they *AREN'T*) we don't realize that we actually have a choice or another option—at least not until something happens, maybe in our environment, that produces a different neuro-response and then suddenly everything is okay. Has this ever happened to you? Has there been a time when, all of a sudden, something takes your mind off your bad mood, like something funny happens and you start cracking up, and then the world doesn't seem so bleak anymore when only three minutes ago, it felt like the world was going to end?

These moments when we get a glimpse of feeling better immediately say everything about what we need to do to get out and stay out of the RB as much as possible. And these moments reveal a method that can help free us from the RB. This is when the good news shows up!

The groundbreaking research I was referring to at the beginning of the chapter wasn't that we are locked in our RB by solidified neural pathways for the rest of our lives—that would make for a horrible book! The groundbreaking research was the discovery that the brain is pliable; it can be changed!

There are so many people out there struggling with mental health symptoms, feeling lousy and thinking there is something wrong with them, that they are damaged or broken. But the reality is these feelings are just symptoms telling you that your reptilian brain has gotten so strong from use that it is just dominating *right now*. And because we know the brain is pliable this means there is something you can do about it!

Studies on neuroplasticity have shown that fundamentally the brain is a muscle, and like any muscle, it gets stronger with use and weaker with a lack of use. What was discovered through neuroscience, and what I have found over the last two decades in my own clinical work, is that we can start to undo the strength of neural pathways in the lower brain by focusing on developing more neural pathways in other parts of the brain.

What is the higher brain?
How can it help us?

There are key strategies that can be done to aid you in getting out of the RB sooner than later. The first step in that direction is learning more about the part of the brain that produces the opposite emotional experience of the RB, and for our purposes in this book, I will refer to this part as the *higher brain*. The higher brain, or HB, is the executive part of the brain that has responses like problem solving, perspective, big picture thinking, assessing consequences, logic, hope, and compassion. This is the part of the brain that is activated when we are feeling good in general, and therefore, it will be vital to strengthen this part of the brain so it can dominate over the lower brain, and we can live in this place more often than not. This will ultimately aid us in being able to access this place when our amygdala gets triggered instead of our RB taking over. And it will teach us how to live in our higher brain vs our lower brain long term. Now the next question of course is, how?

If you went to a personal trainer and said to them that you'd been working on your calves so much that they were bulging out of control, and because you have focused on your calves, you have neglected your biceps, what do you think they would tell you to do? They would say, "Stop working on your calves and start exercising your biceps." The same goes for the brain, the way to start to lessen the hold of the RB is by strengthening the muscles in your higher brain. Let's look at some examples of higher-brain activities, while exploring the question of how to operationalize these strategies in very practical ways, whether as an intervention to manage difficult emotions in the moment or as prevention so you can live life from your higher brain soon than later and more often than not.

Humor

The easiest and quickest way to get into your higher brain is something that I bet you already do or have done—laugh. It's been discovered that it's next to impossible to be genuinely laughing and in your lower brain.

A few years ago, my daughter was studying day and night to pass her algebra exam, and on the afternoon after the test, she came home completely deflated and emotionally distraught, as she was convinced that she had failed. And what did my husband and I do? We started problem solving right away. We suggested that she could email the teacher for extra credit or learn of other options. With each solution, my daughter became more and more angry, but now the venom was heading our way. I quickly realized she was in her RB (I mean HELLO I teach this stuff!). As my dear husband kept trying to help her, I decided to stay silent and focus on cooking dinner. After a moment, he followed my lead, and the room fell suddenly quiet.

After thinking about different options, I grabbed my phone and pulled up a clip from one of my favorite comedies with Will Ferrell (how can you not laugh at any scene with that guy in it?). It was a silly, three-minute scene, and as I put it in front of her, she looked at me incredibly annoyed and asked what this was about. I said I had meant to show her the clip earlier but forgot, and I hit play. Again, not the time to reason with the RB, it won't listen! It was also not the time to take her attitude seriously, because she was drowning in her lower brain. She started to watch the video, and sure enough, once the clip got to the hilarious, gut-busting part, she started to crack up! We started joking about the scene and completely dismissed any talk of exams or strategies to get a better grade. Once we were well into dinner, she mentioned that she might email her teacher about extra credit and what a good idea that was! Ha! It worked. In this scenario, we see that she was emotional activated, and her RB took over, but once she was able to access her higher brain, she suddenly was able to link her amygdala to her higher brain, which really is the goal. Just like we need the RB for physical survival, we need the higher brain for emotional regulation and processing. And for my daughter, it only took a few minutes to get her into her higher brain where she could discuss solutions to her dilemma.

Believe me, it works quick if you stop engaging in whatever the content is that is triggering you or the other person. If it's the other person that is triggered, the success of this process is contingent on you not getting triggered as well. The mistake we made in the beginning with my daughter was that we tried to engage her in problem solving to help her feel better. But the lower brain can almost never leap up to problem solving without doing another HB activity first—especially because the lower brain thinks it's 100% right already, so no solution is going to trump what it thinks is truth. Therefore, you must "Jedi mind trick" your way out of it somehow. What she needed was time and a stimulus to get her into her higher brain, and humor served this purpose.

Notice that logic also triggered her RB defenses—this is because the lower brain doesn't speak that language, and she naturally became annoyed when we tried to implement logic too soon, as it felt invalidating to her current emotional state. In these moments, you need to either validate the feelings (which we will go into in more depth in the subsequent chapter on emotions) and then shift to the higher brain or go right to the higher brain and hope the intervention works. I also have used this technique in de-escalating numerous clients who were prone to highly aggressive outbursts, and what almost always happened is as soon as the laughter came, they were confused as to why they were so upset to begin with. This is because they shifted into their higher brain where all is clear, well, and hopeful.

It's important to make note that this shift can actually feel disorienting at times because there is some awareness of the contrast of how you felt or thought before and how you feel or think after. The disorientation actually means that you were able to change your mind—literally!

Exercises

Now let's explore how humor can help to get you in your HB from your lower brain and work toward completely reorganizing your mind!

Name three ways you can access humor:

1. _____
2. _____
3. _____

Along these lines, write about the last time, or the most significant time, you laughed hard (I have a really funny family, so this one always works for me):

_____
_____
_____
_____
_____

Now how do you feel? _____

> *"You cannot solve a problem from the same state of mind that created it."*
> — Albert Einstein

Hopes and dreams

Neuro-linguistic programing (NLP) is founded on discoveries in brain science that show how to rewire the brain, thereby supporting individuals in decreasing mental health symptoms and feeling better overall. One such study focused on how to help people shift out of their lower brain into their higher brain. Researchers studied participants by hooking their brain up to electrodes to get a clear picture of which parts of the brain responded when asked specific questions and how shifts in mood impact neural activity. First, they had subjects come in and rate their current mood. Then they studied subjects who reported severe anxiety, depression, and suicidal ideation. With these folks, predicably, what they found when they first did imaging was that their lower brain was completely lit up, while the rest of the brain was inactive. From there, they wanted to discover if they could help them experience positive emotions, and if so, how and what happens in the brain in tandem.

After a few trials, they asked the participants to tell them about their hopes and dreams. For example, they asked, "If you were living your ideal life, the life of your dreams, what would that look like?" As each subject responded, guess what happened to their brain? It lit up like a Christmas tree, and they reported a subsequent relief in their symptoms. Further, the higher brain lit up even when the subjects were asked the question, before they answered, which led researchers to assert first that the brain can't resist a question and second that visualizations have the power to activate the higher brain without the subject overtly doing anything. This led researchers to concluded that the brain, in some ways, cannot tell the difference between a visual and reality. That is, when we visualize our dreams, our brain responds as if it's really happening. This makes sense, because regardless of how it happens, when we are in higher brain, the neurotransmitters dopamine (happiness), and serotonin (peace) are automatically released. This means, if we are thinking good thoughts, our brain secretes chemicals that produce and support that feel-good feeling just like it would if we were actually having a pleasant experience out in the world. This study was groundbreaking because it implicated that we can literally influence our neurochemistry by what we are thinking.

I like to joke that we are walking pharmaceutical companies. But I don't think I'm that far off. We have a lot more power over how we feel than we ever imagined—it's just a matter of understanding what we need to do to feel better.

Exercises

Let's have you practice right now by getting in touch with your hopes and dreams!

If I could wave a magic wand and your life suddenly became the life of your dreams, what would that look like and how would it feel?

_____

_____

_____

_____

_____

Now how do you feel? _____

I had a time in my life where my lower brain took over, and predictably, I was experiencing depression and anxiety. I had a close call with my physical health, and it made me go back to my roots. When I did, I remembered that what I think about and focus on everyday influences how I feel in my body, and it also influences my body's health. I couldn't believe that I forgot to implement my higher-brain daily practices because I knew better. Instead of beating myself up about it, I just buckled down and started visualizing. The first thing I visualized was a time in my life when I felt on fire: it was a time that I was so excited about life that in the morning, I would jump out of bed to see what the universe or God had in store for me that day. I remembered how good it felt to be in my body, how free and hopeful and inspired I felt. I did this visual every morning, right before bed, whenever I had a spare moment in the day, and anytime negativity started to creep in. Do you know what happened?

I started to have the same ideal life again! After a while, I was suddenly pulled to make decisions that subtly changed my life and aligned it with the life I was living a decade earlier. Before I knew it, I was that person again because she is me and I am her and she is my potential that I can access at any time. You also have that in you, too.

> *"The more you see yourself as what you'd like to become, and act as if what you want is already there, the more you'll activate those dormant forces that will collaborate to transform your dream into reality."*
> — Wayne Dyer

Remember a time in your life where you felt amazing, on fire, in touch with yourself, or really at peace with life. We usually have at least one time in our life that we can think of that fits this description. And if for some reason you haven't tapped into that yet, no worries—you can still imagine yourself living your best life. Just ask yourself how you would feel and who you would be.

With this exercise, what I want you to do is visualize this a few times a day, and when you visualize it, be sure to feel the feelings associated with it. This, by the way, is the most important part, because the feelings of positivity literally confirm you are in the HB.

Use the space below to record some of the details of this time in your life and be as emotionally descriptive as possible and feel it like it's truly happening again now:

_____

_____

_____

_____

_____

_____

_____

_____

_____

_____

The "I love" list

Okay, the next one, I know, sounds corny but, boy, does it work. This is where you quite simply write out or visualize ten things you absolutely love. Now, it can be anything except addictions—these are more of what keep us stuck in the RB—so don't include on your list things like, drugs, video games, TV, gambling, shopping, and so on. Some examples include a place, event, season, sport, hobby, experience—basically if you really love it when you think about it and it's not an addiction, it qualifies. Think about the thing and then pair it with a salient memory, and again, hone into how it felt to live the experience. For example, if you love the mountains, think about the last time you were in the mountains and relive that experience for a moment. Do this with each item, and I guarantee by the time you reach four, you will start feeling better.

I implemented this as a crisis intervention technique with a client when I was working at a group home for developmentally impaired adult males who had come from a locked facility due to aggressive and unsafe behaviors. On this particular day, I got to the home and one of the residents (I will call him Jose to protect confidentiality) was having an aggressive episode. When Jose saw me, he said, "Aimee, I don't care if I go back to prison, I hate this place and everyone here. I have to get out of this place now, and I'm going to start with throwing furniture." I first validated his feelings, as I knew I couldn't jump right to an HB activity without getting him engaged. I then suggested we go outside so he could smoke. He reluctantly agreed. Once we were there, I asked him to tell me ten things he loved. He was very resistant and again emphasized how much he hated it there and wanted to leave or destroy the entire house to get out. But I, again, validated him and pressed him for at least five things he loved. He started to share: "I love snowboarding. I love spaghetti. I love going to the beach . . ." I interrupted him and asked for a memory for each one, and he complied. He went through last to first. "I love the beach, and the last time I went there I was with my dad and my sister." By the time he got to five, he was smiling ear to ear. I stopped him and asked how he felt. He then looked confused and said, "Wow, I feel good." I smiled and said, "Of course you do." When we think about what we love, we are in our higher brain—and *boom*, it was truly as simple and as quick as that.

Exercises

Now it's your turn. Name ten things that you love and pair each with a vivid memory:

1. _____

_____

2. _____

_____

3. _____

_____

4. _____

_____

5. _____

_____

6. _____

_____

7. _____

_____

8. _____

_____

9. _____

_____

10. _____

_____

_____

Now how do you feel? _____

Gratitude

I once heard that the highest vibration emotions are love and gratitude. In fact, I think the two are intimately tied, because when we shift to a grateful place, we are literally filled with appreciation and love. Now, this shift sometimes isn't felt right away, but if you were to practice gratitude daily for just a week, I bet you would start to see a difference.

There are a couple techniques I have used to feel gratitude, and I am currently doing both:

- a gratitude list
- an end-of-the-day gratitude meditation

Every morning, I make my gratitude list: I set aside five to ten minutes to list ten things I am grateful for (this could also be done at any time, but the mornings really set the tone for the day) and why I am grateful for them. For example, "I am so grateful for my dogs, because they fill me with so much love and laughter." The reason why you tack on the "why" is because it really amplifies the feeling; when we just name the thing, like "I'm so grateful for my dogs," it remains kind of flat. It is key that we feel good when we do this, and by feeling good, we are naturally getting up in the HB and getting flooded with all of our feel-good neurotransmitters.

The other form of gratitude I practice is a nightly gratitude meditation. This is where you grab a rock (maybe pick one out in the garden or maybe you have a special one already) and rub it as you close your eyes and review your day. I think the rock is a good addition, because it really helps to keep you present so your mind doesn't wander too much. As you are reviewing your day, starting from the beginning, only look for the positive experiences you had and really focus on how good those positive experiences felt. When you find one and zone in on the feel-good experience, express your gratitude for it. Then, once you finish your review of the day, go back and pick out the best thing that happened and amplify how good it felt, as well as your sense of gratitude, by saying, "Thank you, thank you, thank you." Each time I do this, a sense of peace comes over me that is palpable.

Exercises

Now you try—list ten things you are grateful for and don't forget the "why."

1. _____
_____
_____

2. _____
_____
_____

3. _____
_____
_____

4. _____
_____
_____

5. _____
_____
_____

6. _____
_____
_____

7. _____
_____
_____

8. _____
_____
_____

9. _____
_____
_____

10. _____
_____
_____

Now how do you feel? _____

Looking forward

Similarly, to our hopes and dreams, this is a simple thing we can do at any point during our day, and it involves focusing on what you are looking forward to. When I was in my twenties, I had a mentor say that you always need to have something on the calendar you are looking forward to, even if it's just dinner with a friend. It's vital to have things that can pull us through tough moments, and tiny little events that we can anticipate with excitement really do the trick.

I used to do this with my daughter when she was young. If she was upset about something or ruminating on the negative for too long, I would start to talk about upcoming events, like Jordynn's birthday party or our summer trip to Tahoe, and she would shift! It just gave her brain something else to focus on, and it was instantly reinforcing, because she started to feel better.

Exercises

Now it's your turn to try. Name three things you are looking forward to (if you haven't planned anything, then name three things you will plan for in the future):

1. _____
2. _____
3. _____

Meditation

Okay, you had to know this one would come up. A study was done that showed if you were to meditate five days a week for just ten minutes, after a year, your brain would be completely rewired—with more neural pathways in your higher brain. Most people try meditation a few times and decide it isn't for them because they can't turn their mind off, but the reality is that if your mind remains active and chatty while meditating, it simply means you are in the right place!

Meditation is a practice, and like any skill, it takes time to be developed. The point of meditation is to help you manage the mental chatter, so the practice doesn't expect you to have that skill already mastered. It would be like going to batting cages for the first time and being upset that you don't know how to bat—that's the whole point of being there! It's the same with meditation, so remind yourself that with practice you will start to learn how to ease your mind and relax into a higher-brain place.

Like with any skill, it takes time. It is truly about learning to accept your thoughts—and if there is mental chatter, don't get caught up in trying to change it and don't freak out because the chatter is there. The goal is to find a place of peace and acceptance regardless of what your thoughts are doing. Also, if you have never meditated before, I highly recommend using one of the many apps out there to guide you. It's useful to begin with structured meditation as you are building the skill, and then you could do more free form after your practice has become more developed.

> *"The goal of meditation isn't to control your*
> *thoughts, it's to stop letting them control you."*
> — Author Unknown

This is not only a vital activity to incorporate into your daily practices, but it is also a great coping skill to use during moments of anxiety or stress. I can't tell you how many times at the end of my day, I have felt anxious and overwhelmed. Having a filled-to-the-brim private practice can do that, but I know if I escape for ten minutes and do my meditation, I am immediately grounded back inside myself again.

Think of it this way, there is an oceanic place of peace inside all of us—we just need the time and space to connect with that place, and then suddenly, no matter what is happening around us, we become the eye of the storm. It's like coming home. And once we develop a solid practice, as soon as we are feeling off balance, we can go in quickly and connect with that sense of peace. Meditation is such a good way to ground ourselves from whatever is happening in the world and connect us with a part of ourselves that is grounded and unshakably flexible.

If you have anxiety, it is literally the one thing I would recommend you do more than anything else. And quite simply, regardless of your mental health symptoms, if you asked me today, "Aimee, what is one thing I can do to change my life?" I would say, "Meditate."

I believe this is why many traditions recommend doing it daily if possible. This is also why if you go to the emergency room complaining of chest pains, only to find out you are having a panic attack, the doctor will likely recommend a few things—and one is meditation. How is that for East meets West?

Random acts of kindness or service to others

Another way to feel better and be in your higher brain is by going out and focusing on other people. In my 20s I had debilitating depression. I had experienced a major trauma years before and hadn't really begun to even start to heal from it. This was also a time when I was finishing school and gathering my intern hours. I'll never forget the disparity in my mood between how I felt before I left to intern and how I felt after I was done. When I was working with others, I felt a complete shift from utter despair to inspiration. Helping other people feel heard and supported did something to me that just lifted my entire being. In fact, I would leave those sessions so moved I would feel on top of the world, even though the morning before my internship I was in a low, depressed place. What I realized pretty quickly was that focusing on other people gave me a break from focusing on myself and all of a sudden I felt like my life had meaning and purpose. Giving to others simply increases our feel-good feelings, so when you do it, you will walk away feeling immediately better. Some ideas for this are to go buy a random stranger a coffee or maybe let someone in front of you during rush hour commute, or open a door randomly for someone, or even go so far as volunteering somewhere. Whatever the gesture, acts of service are really a fulfilling way to activate your higher brain. If you develop a practice of service, you will feel the difference the days you do it as well as the days you don't. Giving to others has the immediate effect of lifting our spirit. And I think in the end life is more about giving than anything else.

Coping skills versus distractions

Almost any coping skill that you enjoy will get you into your higher brain. The feeling of enjoyment is a dead giveaway, and I say "almost any" because it can't be an activity that is a distraction. The difference between the two is whether it connects you more or less to yourself.

Distractions keep us from ourselves, whereas healthy coping skills integrate us with ourselves. Take, for example, video games, they are a lot of fun to play, and they engage you, but you are hardly connecting more to yourself (not to mention, they also manipulate your dopamine levels, which is a whole other discussion, but not healthy if engaged in for too many hours a day). Same goes for social media, TV, drinking, or shopping. It's important to note that distractions are important to have in our lives too—we need to have activities that help us escape the moment so we can disengage from stressful situations at times. Also, distractions can give us the psychological distance necessary to regulate our emotions.

Let's take one of my favorite distractions, watching Netflix on my bed. There are many days after a full caseload that I am simply brain dead, so after doing my coping skills for the day, I unapologetically get emerged in a bingeworthy series. I love it, but if I do it too much or if I negate my other coping strategies, I start to feel sluggish and unmotivated, which is a message telling me I need to reach for more substantive activities. It would be like eating desert all day long without consuming anything with real nutrients: over time, you are going to start to feel unhealthy. This is what it feels like on a psychological level with too many distractions. Further, if we use a distraction over and over again as a means of coping and self-soothing, it will become an addiction. This is when we come to believe consciously or unconsciously that we need it to feel better.

Another thing to note is there are some healthy coping skills that, to the excess, can fall under the distraction/addiction category too. Take working out for example, if we work out too much, the activity is likely leaning more toward an addiction, which could become self-destructive. Whatever it is, once we start "using" the activity because we think it's going to fill the void inside of us or it's going to rescue us from what we are feeling deep down, it becomes an addiction and something we believe we need to function. The reality is the void and difficult emotions that lie inside are created and/or perpetuated *by* distracting ourselves from our current experience to begin with.

Healthy coping strategies connect us more to ourselves which can provide a method for grounding us while enabling us to integrate emotional material, which will lead to healing and wholeness. So, in the interest of growth and psychological health, connection to self is the ultimate goal. However, this can become tricky for someone who has experienced a lot of traumas; for this individual there is a lot of pain inside, so going in and connecting to themselves is something they have sought to avoid. For this individual, instead of feeling their emotions, which were/are way too overwhelming and layered, it has become vital to distract and numb themselves from what lies inside. In fact, after experiencing a trauma, it's absolutely necessary for anyone to distance themselves from emotional material because it's just too big and too overwhelming to process.

Elizabeth Kubler-Ross said: "Denial [and repression] helps us to pace feeling our grief. There is grace in [them]. It is nature's way of letting in only as much as we can handle." Know that whatever distractions you use that may have become more addictive in nature, you developed this strategy as a way to survive. If we can honor our distractions, as dysfunctional as they may turn out to be, from a place of understanding, acceptance, and compassion, then we can start to discern how to lessen our reliance on our distractions and integrate more activities that connect us.

So know that if you have been using distractions to cope up until this point, it is okay and totally normal, but hopefully, with the exercises in this book, along with the chapter on healing, you will develop a healthier balance between your coping skills and your distractions. In the end, the more we are in our higher brain, the better we feel, and healthy coping skills naturally get us up there.

Exercises

Before we explore healthy coping activities, what are some activities that you do that fall under the distraction category? (No judgement—again, we all need a few distractions as a go-to.)

1. _____
2. _____
3. _____
4. _____
5. _____
6. _____

Activities that fall under the category of healthy coping skills are things like music (listening/playing/writing), singing, dancing, writing, drawing, exercise in moderation (any form), walking, hiking, being out in nature, riding a bike, building things, cleaning out drawers/closets (without going to the extreme), looking at the stars, and so on. These tend to be the activities that maybe we have always enjoyed since childhood.

For me riding my bike and writing poems filled my cup when I was a kid, but when I got older, I forgot all about my bike—that is until my twenties, which is when I started doing deeper healing work on myself. After exploring what coping activities were natural to me, I rediscovered the joy of riding my bike again. When I do it, I literally feel like I did in my youth, safe, grounded and at peace, which is exactly what we are looking for here. Many clients I have worked with get stumped on this one, they aren't sure what they enjoy. This just means you have forgotten, but no worries—the answers are inside of you. If you think back to your childhood, what did you love to do? It's almost as easy as that.

Take a few moments to mediate on this and then write down what you come up with below:

1. _____
2. _____
3. _____
4. _____

5. _____

6. _____

Just three things

Over the years, I've learned that the changes we make really hinge less on one big ah-ha moment and more on the things we do daily to either encourage our growth and healing or discourage our growth and healing; they either connect us to ourselves or disconnect us. What you do every day completely matters in how you feel—it's almost everything.

I have now developed what I call daily practices to really support me in filling my inner cup and staying in my higher brain. Daily practices are simply effective coping strategies. I have really come to terms with the reality that we need to be implementing activities daily that hook us into our higher brain. For me, when I first did these activities, I didn't notice a huge difference so much, but, boy, once I quit doing them, the reality set in—what I do with my time either connects me to myself, my source, and the light, or it disconnects me. With this in mind, I started to zero in on what practices were the most fulfilling and satisfying to my nature, and what I stumbled on was the idea of "just three things."

These three things fall under the categories of body, mind, and spirit. To break it down, we have doing something to:

1. invigorate the body
2. inspire the mind or channel/engage our emotions
3. connect with our spirit or the place of peace inside

Let me elaborate on each:

Body: This is obvious—it's doing something physical, something that feels good for our body in the long run. For example, running, swimming, walking, power yoga, riding your bike, or working out.

Mind/Emotions: This category can be anything that stimulates the mind like listening to inspirational podcasts, reading, writing, or doing anything that accesses emotions, like creative or expressive activities (so art of any kind), singing, dancing, journaling, and so on.

Spirit: This one is the one that stumps most people, especially if you're not spiritual or religious. But have no fear, this category is just about seeking a sense of peace and/or meaning, which includes activities like meditation, being in nature, listening to calming music, looking at the stars, practicing yoga (which can go here or under the body section), reading something that deeply resonates, looking up inspirational quotes, reading spiritual or religious texts, or any activity that hits that peaceful feeling. I also think acts of service would go well here too, because service helps us tap into a greater sense of purpose, which I think is the realm of the soul as well.

Now the trick is figuring out which three things are really going to fit the bill for you. Maybe you notice that you have more than one activity for a category—that's awesome! The most important thing is to just pick one from each area every day and practice them.

> *"You'll never change your life until you change*
> *something you do daily. The secret of your success is*
> *found in your daily routine."*
> — John Maxwell

My three things currently are: (1) working out/doing yoga or riding my bike, (2) reading inspirational literature, writing/journaling, gratitude list (one of the three), and (3) meditating. What I have noticed is that if I do three of my activities daily, I feel grounded and connected to myself. If I only do two, I still feel pretty good, but not as on fire. And if I only do one, forget it—I'm more prone to anxiety, succumbing to stress, and more vulnerable to negative thinking. It really is this simple.

I had a client who came in complaining of intrusive thoughts that were highly debilitating. He was open to absolutely anything (which I personally love as a therapist!), and through collaboration, he came up with his "just three things." These were (1) exercise, (2) gratitude list, and (3) meditation. After about three months of him implementing his daily practices, he told me that he couldn't understand it, but his ruminating thoughts had completely calmed down. I asked about his practices, and he said, "No way; it can't be that." He thought it had to have been his life circumstances.

So, I said, "okay, we will see how it goes". Since he was doing better, we scheduled the next session a few weeks out.

A few weeks later, he came back in declaring that he was now doing horribly, his intrusive thoughts had returned, and his negative life circumstances had also resurfaced. I, of course, asked about his practices, and he admitted that he had stopped meditating and doing his gratitude list as he didn't feel like he needed them anymore. I said, "Okay, let's have you try it again and we'll see how you do." He agreed and again came back a few weeks later. Sure enough, he came in and said, "Well, it's a miracle, but my thoughts have calmed again... but my circumstances have also improved, so that's got to be it." I asked about his practices, and he responded, "Oh yea, I've been doing them but I don't think it has anything to do with the shift in my mood, it's got to be my circumstances."

At this point, I just giggled. This went on for almost three years, back and forth: one week, he'd feel great and be mediating and doing his other practices, and then another week, he would stop and feel horrible. After enough time, he started to admit there definitely was a correlation: he reluctantly came to concede that these practices seemed to do "something"! And this made me giggle a bit louder.

I give this example not only to highlight how subtle the changes will likely be—you won't even think it's tied to what you are doing—but also to highlight the phenomena that when you start to change on the inside, things also change on the outside. Each time he was doing good, his circumstances also improved. Mystics have always known, and quantum physics has shown, that there is a direct correlation between our energy and how the environment responds to us. When you change how you feel, you also change the way you see the world around you. This makes sense even considering your facial expressions and posture: it indicates to the world if you are at peace or in distress, and it seems like the universe follows suit.

> *"Change the way you look at things and the things you look at will change."*
> — Wayne Dyer

The goal is to keep doing things that make you feel good and keep your energy high, and then the world around you will respond in kind. And if you don't feel good and your energy is low, know that the low energy, negative life encounters, and mental health symptoms are likely messengers telling you that you need to be doing something different with your time.

In my life, whenever I start to feel not so great, I always stop and think, *Wait, what have I been doing or not doing?* Sure enough I always respond with, *Oh, that's right, I stopped . . .* (fill in the blank: meditating, writing, etc.). The good news is once you know the ingredients for your feel-good state, it's as easy as implementing them once again, and within a few weeks (maybe sooner), you will start to notice a spring in your step!

Exercises

Let's have you list out what your "just three things" are that you want to start implementing or maybe continue implementing to see if they are the ingredients for your sense of peace and well-being (you can put more than one activity in each category, too). Remember it's all field research ☺.

My "just three things" are:

1. Body_____
2. Mind/Emotions_____
3. Spirit_____

Back to the reptilian brain

The exercises we just explored give you potential strategies to activate your higher brain. Ideally, what will happen is the daily practices and coping skills that work for you will become clearer. It's vital to use the higher brain as much as possible because the brain is a muscle, and if you want to lessen the reptilian brain's hold on the rest of the brain, you must start to strengthen the higher brain. Like any muscle, it gets stronger with use. So, the key is going to be practice, practice, practice because the more you use it the stronger it gets and the more it will dominate.

Another key element to higher-brain activities is to use them in moments of emotional activation. If the lower brain is incited into fight, flight, or freeze and yet physical danger is not imminent, you need to do something to mitigate the false flag triggering of the RB. What I have discovered in these moments is that you really have two options:

1. Get out of the RB immediately or
2. Process.

Let's explore the first option in a little more depth.

On our way to exploring Option 1 (get out of the RB immediately), let's walk through the process again. Something happens and *bam*—you are triggered and in your RB. Before you do anything, the first most important step in navigating the RB is knowing that you are in the RB. Again, this part of the brain, when activated, will tell you that what you are feeling and thinking is 100% accurate, so you won't really believe you are in the RB at first. Therefore, learning to catch when you are triggered and in the RB is the first goal—but not an easy feat.

When activated, the RB naturally drives our awareness underground, because fight, flight, or freeze hinges on reflexive knee-jerk responses that necessarily operate beneath or outside our conscious awareness. The way I have come to know I'm in this part of the brain is by the quality of my thoughts: I've pretty much made a deal with myself that if I use the words "always," "never," "nobody," "everybody," coupled with a negative view of the future, present, and past—I'm there. Also, I know that if suddenly I'm only thinking about my husband's negative traits (my poor husband!) and he's now the worst human on earth, I'm also definitely there (especially if five minutes ago, he was my best friend). In these moments, because a lot of times our triggers can be subtle, I give myself a reality test, and if I check any of the RB boxes above, then I know I can't take my thoughts seriously. From there, I have my go-to strategies to get out of this part of the brain.

Exercises

Before we move to the getting out of RB part of the process, let's have you explore your RB cues. Think about the last time you were really triggered and examine your thoughts (things like "always," "never," "nobody," "everybody"), feelings, or physical sensations (maybe your internal temperature increases, your heart races, or your mind gets foggy). Write these below so you can increase your awareness of the cues of your RB:

1. _____
2. _____
3. _____
4. _____
5. _____
6. _____
7. _____
8. _____
9. _____

Back to the first piece of the puzzle: once you learn how to identify that you are in RB, the next step is learning how to get out of RB immediately (if possible). A vital thing to note here is that if you are in the RB because you are triggered in your interaction with someone, the first thing to do is take a time-out (which we will go more into detail later in the chapter dealing with relationships and triggers). There are no conversations to be had from the lower brain: it will all be negative and likely will result in a fight with the other person. And then once on a time out then you can focus on strategies that will aid you in activating your higher brain thereby getting out of your lower brain ASAP and gaining access to problem solving and conflict resolution strategies. If your trigger wasn't in response to an interaction with someone in the moment the goal most of the time, no matter what instigated the RB response, is to seek a way up into the higher brain to feel better and gain perspective.

For me, when I identify that I'm in the RB, I *force myself* to go for a walk, meditate, find something funny (YouTube videos or memes), listen to inspirational books/podcasts. or do some yoga. I say, *'force myself'* because again when I'm in RB I don't always want to believe I'm there- my ego/RB kicks in and says, 'no Aimee, what you are feeling is true'. But luckily, I have now learned that if I check a lot of the cues to my RB boxes, I know I'm there and after doing this work on myself for a couple of decades I have a lot of successful go-to activities that really work.

The journey will be for you to discover what higher brain techniques work for you when you are activated, so allow this process to take time. Humor is a common strategy my clients implement as well as finding something inspirational to listen to (quotes, podcasts or even audiobooks). Ask yourself what could work for you? And then know that you may have to develop a habit through trial and error to have it become a viable option. Let's take a moment and have you list out below some strategies that you think might be helpful:

1. _____
2. _____
3. _____
4. _____
5. _____
6. _____

Again, the most challenging part of this process is the fact that when we are in the RB, we don't want to do anything productive. In fact, all we want to do is destroy things or create more negativity. My then eleven-year-old daughter put it best when she described her experience of navigating the RB by saying, "Mama, I'm getting really good at knowing when I'm in reptilian brain, but when I'm there, I still don't want to get out." How true this statement is!

When we are in the RB, we feel justified for being there, so getting out, or better yet, having the motivation to get out can be a challenge. For many, the trick is forcing yourself to *do something* higher brain and not to continue operating and interacting from your lower brain. You must remind yourself that these thoughts aren't rooted in truth; it's as simple as that. And once you start to catch yourself in your RB, you will get better and better at navigating your way through it, because you are literally creating, and through repetition, solidifying new neural pathways each time you do it. Because of this solidification, over time, it will get easier. Like developing any new behavior, the beginning is the hardest part but if you practice your coping strategies consistently you will start to build momentum.

Also, remember, when we are in fight, flight, or freeze—we are in a panicked place neurologically, and there is an impulse to act to save ourselves.

However, there is no lion to slay and no danger to run from, and since there is nothing to do, we are still compelled to act somehow, which can be a problem. How many times have you gotten triggered at work and just wanted to quit or got in a fight with your partner and just wanted to end the relationship? I'm sure it's happened to many of you; I know it's sure happened to me, and I will tell you, the most important thing to know about the RB is, whatever you do, DON'T MAKE ANY LIFE CHANGING DECISIONS.

Remind yourself that the RB is only 2% of your brain, so doing anything major will likely lead to regret. Many of the couples I've worked with tend to break up when in the RB, and sure enough, the moment they come out of it, they always say, "Shoot, what did I just do?" I always tell my couples, if you want to break up, no problem, just wait until you feel that way for thirty days straight, when you have at least been in a higher mood on some of those days, and if you still feel that way, then by all means make a run for it!

Now that we have reviewed the 1st option for when you are triggered and in RB (i.e., getting out of RB immediately), we turn to the 2nd option, which is to process.

For option two, when there is nothing that can get me out of the reptilian brain, I know that I may need to process some emotion that is beneath the surface. What this means is that what triggered me likely brought up repressed emotions and it's time to process some of that emotional material which translates to: it's time to have a good cry. When our higher brain strategies are not working, it is likely time to feel and only through processing emotions on a deeper level, will you be able to shift back up to your higher brain with higher brain strategies. This is what the processing options equates to.

This phenomenon brings us to the next vital piece of the puzzle that serves as a bit of a snag in the entire process of feeling better long term. Because in order to free ourselves from the reptilian brain hold and to live in our higher brain consistently we need to heal what brought us down to our lower brain to begin with. This brings us to the next topic: healing what needs to heal.

A wrinkle to higher brain activation: the need to heal

There is an exception to the notion that all we must do is strengthen the higher brain to disarm the hold of the reptilian brain. While this is a fundamental piece in undoing and loosening the RB's rule, and usually successful for helping us feel better in the moment, it isn't the complete antidote for breaking the neural pathways that binds us to our reptilian brain once and for all.

The piece that is just as vital and I think often gets missed with more modern therapeutic approaches is healing the trauma that created the reptilian brain's neural pathways to begin with. Think of it like scar tissue—when we go through a trauma, we get a highly solidified neural pathway that happens in concert with our reaction to the trauma. When the trauma moment happens the amygdala activates the RB intensely and it's like the intensity imprints so deeply, the highly solidified neural pathway becomes like scar tissue that binds the amygdala and RB. This figurative scar tissue is one of the reasons why we have triggers later in life and it is also a reason why we become stuck in the RB and end up developing mental health symptoms. How we adapt and survive our trauma becomes literally embedded in the crevices of our brain, and while this is happening neurologically, it's also happening emotionally. What we do to survive trauma at the psyche level is to repress most, and sometimes all, the emotions that were ignited by the trauma—again, when the RB is activated, all other facilities shut down, including our ability to emotionally respond to the situation. This results in the repression of emotions which is the scar tissue equivalent in the psyche. And it is the figurative scar tissue in the brain and in the psyche that are at the root of our triggers and mental health symptoms.

I have come to view the repression of emotions and solidified neural pathways as being transfixed together until the individual's psyche feels "safe" enough to start to heal and until it feels safe enough for us to start breaking up that scar tissue. So, the wrinkle is that we must heal from the traumas that created the RB's hold to live life from the higher brain consistently, thereby freeing ourselves from mental health symptoms, like anxiety, depression, rage, triggers, OCD, and addictions, to name a few. And the scar tissue is not just neurological, it's emotional.

We can work toward developing higher-brain dominance over the lower brain, but we will always be pulled back down to the RB if we don't heal the emotional piece as well. Processing our emotions is the equivalent of breaking up that scar tissue. And when we do this emotionally alongside building higher brain neural pathways, it also frees up the neural pathway solidification in the brain as well.

When I was in my 20s, I learned all about coping skills and higher brain activities, and I got really good at doing my daily practices. There were times that I felt pretty good for a while, but then my depression would surface again. It was a cycle until I started to recognize that I could build new neural pathways and have healthy higher brain strategies all I want, but I would always be pulled back down to the lower brain until I truly healed the emotional wounds that created the lower brain neural pathways to begin with. And it was when I started to do the deeper, emotional work that my depression started to lessen for good.

Let's explore the process of emotional repression and healing and how it ties with the reptilian brain and solidified neural pathways by delving more deeply into the nature of emotions themselves.

CHAPTER 2
Emotions, Repression, and Healing

What are emotions really?

For most of us, we are taught not to take our emotions too seriously, and for almost all of us, we are taught that to be a mature and valued human being, we better learn how to control them. But is it even possible to completely control our emotions or, even better, to control our emotions without consequences?

If we look at the word itself, we can get to the root of what emotions are linguistically—they are energies that want to move: *e*-motion. Through my own experiences, I have come to see that an emotion is emotive energy that has a specific path of expression it naturally wants to follow to be released, which goes something like:

1. *Impetus:* An emotion is ignited in response to something occurring inside or outside us.
2. *Movement with the body:* It makes its way through the body (e.g., when we start to feel sad, we might first feel it in our stomach or our chest, and then maybe our throat expands, our eyes soften, our lip quivers—getting ready for the outward expression of crying).
3. *Expression:* We outwardly express the emotion, like crying and then verbalizing what is wrong.
4. *Environmental witnessing:* Our emotion is heard and seen by others.
5. *Validation:* The emotion is received by our environment, and we are given validation for the emotion (e.g., "Of course, you're sad.

Your best friend is moving away"). This validation provides the vital feedback that says it's okay to feel and express this, and you are not crazy for feeling or expressing this. This step encourages us to let the emotion move outward. (Note: We really need this from our environment growing up, but as adults, we can learn to do this for ourselves.)

6. *Understanding*: We achieve understanding as to why we are feeling what we are feeling. The understanding comes more easily when we are validated, because it says it's okay to continue feeling what we feel, which will make it easier for us to look within to get more insight into our feelings. This is also the step where we don't move to hide it, fade it, or fix it—we understand it's okay to express it.

7. *Acceptance:* We accept that we feel how we feel, and this literally opens us up to allowing the emotion to move through us. We have complete transparency with it—we don't feel ashamed for feeling what we are feeling, and there's no holding down of the emotion. Through this process, we accept our emotional truth.

8. *Surrendering or letting go:* Once we accept our emotional truth, we can then allow the emotion to finish its loop of expression, thereby processing this layer of our emotional reaction to the event. A lot of times what helps with this step is finding a sense of purpose or meaning to the traumatic experience or the incident that created the emotional reaction. When this happens it's almost like the experience wasn't in vain, instead the experience will help us to help the world or other people in some way.

9. *Correct cognitive distortions*: find out what you told yourself about you because of the given experience. A lot of times it's something like this, *'it's all my fault this happened therefore I'm a flawed and horrible human'*, or *'because this happened, I must have deserved it which means I'm inherently bad.'* Also explore what you told yourself about the world, things like: *'People aren't trustworthy, and the world is filled with horrible and selfish people'*…etc. These internal thoughts lead to decisions and become unconscious beliefs (also known as automatic core beliefs – to be discussed in subsequent chapters) later in life which will influence and limit how we see ourselves and

the world, which usually is for the worse. I have found that correct-ing and dissolving these beliefs are a key element to deeper healing and lasting change.

This process sounds easy, right? Going from feeling to expressing to validating to accepting to surrendering and then correcting cognitive dis-tortions all sounds so simple. The reality is that this almost never happens. The emotion usually gets halted for several different reasons. First, if a dif-ficult life experience happens when we are young, we don't have the cogni-tive development to really process the emotion in an insightful way, so the cognitive piece of understanding as well as the last few steps goes undone. In this scenario, maybe the emotion is validated, and we learn we can express it, but the higher-brain understanding isn't achieved, which will require a deeper processing later in life. And as we continue our emotional development, we will have more internal resources to process past traumas more comprehensively.

Also, this is the thing about healing, if we have a trauma or loss, we will always be processing layers of it at different times in life, no matter what. Even when we feel "resolved" with it, in another decade, we might see it differently, which will enable us to process it from another angle and achieve a different level of understanding and more healing. This, in some ways, is the good news about difficult life experiences—the learning is endless. The key is seeing it like that.

I always remind myself that life is a classroom not a fairytale, so learning is the goal. This helps me embrace the ongoing processing of life experi-ences. Now, I do think we get to a lightening, almost emptying, of emotions with certain experiences but we get to add on more insight potentially later in life by continuing to process the event. The older I get the more I see all my traumas from a new lens which means I get to continue to learn and grow.

A second reason an emotion gets halted is when the experience is an intense trauma. As was discussed previously, in this scenario, our brain is automatically in the RB, so it doesn't have the capability to process anything on an emotional level. Remember, in this state, it only has three options—fight, flight, or freeze—so naturally the emotion will need to be repressed. If it wasn't repressed, it would overwhelm our system, distracting us from attending to whatever the threat is in our environment and thus, repression must occur unconsciously, quickly, and necessarily.

And the final reason an emotion is kept from completing its loop of expression is when our environment is not able to provide Step 3 and/ or Step 4 (hearing and seeing the emotion and validating the emotion). This is when we learn that certain emotions cannot be expressed in our environment, which results in halting those emotions in the interest of emotional adaption and survival. I was raised in a Portuguese family, and what that meant in terms of emotional expression was that we could be angry, passive-aggressive, passionate, and joyful, but we could not be sad. Sadness equated weakness and selfishness in my family. In fact, if you came out and expressed sadness, you would hear dismissive comments like, "There are children starving in other countries, what do you have to be sad about?" Now, while this is an attempt at helping us gain perspective and maybe access gratitude, when we are in the middle of feeling something, we can't abandon the path of expression and hop up into the higher brain and access those higher-brain facilities, so instead, we internalize this to mean, "Your feelings don't matter and there is something wrong with you for feeling this way." If you lived in this family when sadness happened, you naturally cut off your emotional expression at Step 3 (expression of emotion) or Step 4 (where the environment witnesses the emotion), because you could not progress to Step 5 (validation of the emotion) in a family that does not value sadness. I unconsciously learned this taboo in my family culture, which resulted in cutting off the emotion of sadness from ever really showing up. Eventually, I got to the point where I stopped feeling it altogether, and over time, this resulted in a split from Step 1 (inception of emotion) to Step 2 (feeling the emotion in my body). I literally got to the point where I couldn't feel much of anything.

"Validation doesn't mean we agree with another's subjective reality. Validation allows another person's emotional state a space to exist."
— Dr. Jamie Long of The Psychology Group

Every family has different taboos around certain emotions, some emotions are welcomed, and others are frowned upon. If we learn that we aren't "allowed" to express a certain emotion, we naturally are going to get good at repressing that emotion in order to adapt to our childhood context. It's what human beings do, and we are so good at it when it happens, we don't even realize we are doing it.

The problem with all of this is the reality that we have a myriad of emotions for a reason. In fact, I believe every emotion communicates something important to us. And if we only learned their language, emotions wouldn't feel so dangerous or unruly. For example, anger often times tells us there is a boundary violation and we need to do something about it, and sadness requires us to soften, mourn, or process a challenging experience. Also, if we allow ourselves to feel what we feel, the funny thing is that our emotions will move. And if we just allow whatever emotion is there to be there, we tap into our emotional truth, and this honesty moves us toward being authentic and whole—which puts us in harmony with our very nature.

We can't just experience one emotion forever, and as much as many cultures aim to be happy all the time, how boring would that be? Not only that, but happy is what it is *because* of sadness—the contrasting emotions define each other. So, if we were always happy, it wouldn't even be happy anymore but the status quo, and being only happy would also be impossible because, well, happy is a verb and, therefore, changeable.

If we aim for honesty and authenticity, I do believe we can experience a sense of peace and contentment that can be at the underpinning of all other emotions that come and go. Take, for example, the blue sky- behind any weather that might be occurring in the immediate environment—whether it is raining or snowing or storming—that blue sky is always there. A sense of peace and calm and feeling grounded can be at the underpinning of your emotions as well, and the way toward actualizing this state of being is by allowing whatever emotion that is present to be there and knowing that the sense of peace and calm is always in the background. Once we realize that we will be okay and the emotion won't stay forever, we get better at allowing our emotions to be there. And ironically, once we allow our emotions to be there and we move through our emotional loop of expression, the emotion starts to fade.

The first step toward emotional authenticity and clearing the scar tissue that binds your lower brain to your amygdala entails an exploration of what emotions you have negated from your current experience. Once you uncover this piece, you will then be on your way toward understanding more of what might be repressed inside. This is the movement toward healing.

> *"Emotional pain is not something that should be hidden away and never spoken about. There is truth in your pain, there is growth in your pain, but only if it's first brought out into the open."*
> — Steven Aitchison

Exercises

Let's stop for a second and have you name what the taboo emotions were/are in your family of origin, and then share what the rules were around that emotion (if you were criticized or ignored etc.). After that, list out the okay emotions below:

Not okay emotion:

    1. _____

What it looked like:

_____

_____

Not okay emotion:

    2. _____

What it looked like:

_____

_____

Not okay emotion:

3. _____

What it looked like:

_____

_____

Okay emotions

1. _____
2. _____
3. _____
4. _____
5. _____

What happens when we can't release our emotions?

Now that we can see why we halted certain emotions, the next question of course is: When an emotion is halted and prevented from completing its loop of expression, what happens next? This is where we go back to the essence of what emotions are: they are energy that want to move. With that in mind, what happens then if you halt energy from moving outward and freeze it in its tracks?

Well, embedded in the first law of thermodynamics is the axiom that states: energy is never lost only transferred. That means, when energy is ignited, it exists and remains in existence—therefore, it must go somewhere, and since it can't move outward, it goes back inside. But instead of it, maybe, evaporating, it remains, and since its energy is now contained, you just figuratively put a lid on a boiling pot of water. Over time, that repressed emotional energy will start to build with more pressure, and just like you would expect when you put a lid on a boiling pot of water, the energy inside will start to intensify and naturally seek ways out, either through steam or an explosion.

In humans, the equivalent of steam and sometimes an explosion is acting-out behaviors, like temper tantrums, aggressive outbursts, or mental health symptoms like anxiety, PTSD, phobias, triggers, or OCD. All these symptoms are merely telling us that there is trapped energy inside that is building with intensity and getting to the point where it is requiring an outlet to release some of its intensity. Take anxiety, for example, and recall what that feels like inside your body, that sense of tightness in the chest or stomach or maybe the tingling sensation in parts of the body and/or racing thoughts. When you really access the somatic memory of it, you can feel the trapped energy. And again as mental health symptoms are a signifier that you are in your RB it's also telling you that you have repressed energy - the two are happening in concert together.

What also happens when we successfully put a lid on our emotions is that over time, we get good at containing *all* our emotions, and eventually, this leads us to not feel any emotions, good or bad, which results in the experience of depression. The very word says what's happening: you are pressing down your emotions (de-pressing) and the resulting lethargy and complete lack of energy you feel is because you are using all your energy to hold your emotions down, resulting in the depletion of energy all together. I have never met a depressed person that openly and consistently shares their feelings—it just doesn't happen. And I know this is why I personally was depressed for over fifteen years. After I learned to repress my sadness at a young age, I then had a serious trauma when I was seventeen, and other resulting traumas, which lead me to completely seal off all my emotions. I got so good at it, I couldn't cry for at least a decade, and I also couldn't feel much of anything else either; joy, excitement, and motivation were all muted.

OCD is also a similar phenomenon, but here, our anxiety latches on to certain thoughts that are purporting to help us, telling us that if we act out certain behaviors, we will achieve relief. But what happens instead is that you stay in the OCD loop and you never achieve relief because you aren't getting to the root of the emotions.

With emotionally reactive acting-out behaviors, like temper tantrums or aggressive episodes, you might be wondering why they do not relieve some emotional repression. The answer is because we aren't hitting Step 6 on the emotional loop of expression—getting insight and understanding into why we are feeling what we are feeling. Most of the time, these episodes are attached to something happening right now, which are merely triggers for historic emotional material. When we act out, we are really expressing emotional energy from yesterday but confusing it with what is happening today, and therefore, no deeper processing is really happening. What often happens is that individual who had the temper tantrum or aggressive outburst might feel better for a while, but once they are done, they just put the lid back on the boiling pot of water and it's only a matter of time before the figurative lid explodes and they act out again.

Also when we have all these incomplete emotional loops resulting in emotional repression inside of us, we again will be suffering from mental health symptoms like depression or anxiety, and over time, we will turn to activities to manage all of this. For many, these turn into addictions. Recall the discussion on distractions turning into addictions? This phenomenon makes sense because all the muck inside of us will eventually demand some type of relief or anesthesia to keep us from feeling what's happening in there—addictions serve this function not only to distract us but to numb us.

> *"I'm not addicted to alcohol or drugs. I'm addicted to escaping reality."*
> — Author Unknown

This is also why, try as we might to develop higher-brain neural pathways, if we don't release our emotional repression, we will always have mental health symptoms creeping back in. What I have learned from my own healing, as well as my clinical observations, is that once we start to heal what needs to heal, we can begin to lessen the scar tissue that connects the amygdala to the reptilian brain, and then we are more able to stay in the higher brain to achieve lasting symptom relief. Feeling what we need to feel and releasing emotionally repressed energy is the way we break up that figurative scar tissue in our minds and in our psyche and this results in true healing.

I have been without depression now for over a decade—but it wasn't until I started to couple my higher brain exercises with deep healing, thereby releasing massive amounts of repressed energy and undoing the deep neural pathway solidification in my brain, that my depression lifted. And then I preventatively started expressing my thoughts and feelings daily so the depression wouldn't resurface. Verbalizing thoughts and feelings are so vital to keep depression from returning. This way, I never hold anything in. What I feel, I express, and I express it as soon as possible.

How do we release our emotional repressions?

To begin the deeper work, we must get clear on what emotional loops and repressed emotional energies are inside. The way toward discovering this information varies from person to person. This is why healing repressed emotions is an art, not a science; I don't think there is any one way of accessing emotions. In fact, I've found that it's different for everyone, but the universals are to:
- remember
- feel
- accept

The acceptance piece is not only accepting what happened but accepting how we feel about what happened. For example, let's say when you were ten your mom was sick with an illness, so when your dog died, she couldn't comfort you. This experience was really upsetting to you deep down and as a child you felt alone and like you mom didn't care about your loss (your now core automatic belief, a term which we will delve into more later). Now, as an adult, you intellectually understand why your mom couldn't be there, and the tendency is to dismiss any negative feelings or hurt because you have forgiven her in your mind, but your emotions haven't been processed. So, in this example, you must get to a place where it's okay that you're sad or mad about the fact that your mom wasn't able to be there for you when you needed her—you need to feel this without justifying why you shouldn't. If you can allow yourself to feel your emotional truth and move toward processing and accepting your emotional truth you can move toward the letting go and ultimate release of the emotion. However, as with most upsetting scenarios in our life we almost always halt the processing of the emotions because in our mind we have already decided to forgive and forget.

> "Sometimes you have to let your heart catch up with your mind..."
> — Author Unknown

What happens frequently in the processing of emotions is that we get to an intellectually mature place with our scars before our emotions have time to be processed, healed, and integrated. We tell ourselves that it's okay that our dad wasn't there or that our mom made the decisions that she did, because we know their background and we know that they did their best with the inner and outer resources they had. We forgive them for any wrongdoing from this reasonable, compassionate place, which is really great and feels healthy. This is a trick, though, because no matter what your mind tells you or what you think is evolved and emotionally mature, you cannot move past your history without honoring your feelings around it, thereby moving your emotions through the loop of expression, and allowing yourself to finally express and release those emotions. Once you do this, the emotional energy will lessen and then you can authentically forgive the person from a mind/emotions place.

Without the emotional work being completed, whatever your mind says about it will be a lie, because your emotions feel something different. The name of the game here is the truth—your *emotional truth*. Asking yourself what is true for you right now with your emotional experience is always the best question. If you can honor whatever is there and allow it to be there and to be felt and expressed, the emotion will shift. And by doing this, you are figuratively riding the current of that emotion and you are giving it space and acceptance so it can complete its loop and move on. The intellectual piece where we see the big picture and forgive is a vital part of the puzzle, too, but we just can't bypass our emotions in favor of it. Likewise, we also can't swim in our emotions 24/7 and blame everyone for what's happened to us either.

I can't highlight enough, that exercises that dig up historic pain that may have been instigated by our caregivers or anyone else aren't designed to place blame on anyone. Instead, they are designed to help you heal your historic scars which don't require you to even confront your caregivers or anyone from the past if that wouldn't be helpful. The deeper work you are doing is internal so *you* can be whole, healed, and, ultimately, release the past once and for all. The goal is to be authentic and whole—blocked energy keeps us from both. Now, many don't want to talk about the past, but if you have historic scars and wounds, the past is actually here. Whether you acknowledge it or not, you are already living in the past by carrying around all of the emotional energy from the past inside you.

I had a major 'ah-ha' moment with the concept of honoring my feelings not that long ago. I was driving and thinking about this minor, and I would say petty, conflict I had experienced in my family a couple years before, and I was disturbed that it still bothered me. I was wrestling with this for a while until I realized that really it bothered me that it bothered me. I suddenly realized that I was stuck with the bothered feeling for way too long, because I wasn't letting the original feeling of being bothered be there. I was covering it with my judgement about it. I got in touch with the feeling of being bothered that it bothered me, and the top bothered (the judgmental feeling of the primary feeling) was almost distracting me from the original feeling of being bothered, which is why I felt stuck. I then was responding to the judgment by scrambling internally to get rid of my primary feeling of being bothered: "Why does it still bother me? What is wrong with me that I can't shake this? I'm a therapist for crying out loud! This shouldn't be affecting me for so long . . ." As you can see, I did what many do with their life experiences—I expected my emotions to catch up with my intellectualized place of acceptance.

At this point, I suddenly realized what was keeping me in a bind. It wasn't the primary feeling of being bothered, but the secondary feeling that wasn't allowing the primary feeling to be there without judgement;

without trying to hide it, fade it, or fix it. And I was doing all three of these internally. Once I took the top emotion off and allowed the primary emotion of being bothered to remain, the primary emotion started to fade. I noticed by the end of the day, the intensity was greatly diminished, and this was when it hit me—we must acknowledge and accept the truth of our emotional experience. If we can accept the truth, acknowledge it, and allow it to be there, then the emotion moves- again freeing it to move along the loop of expression pathway.

What I have come to realize is that emotions are never wrong—their very existence makes them true. Like I said before, it's what we do about them that can be "right" or "wrong." Our tendency to deal with our emotions like we would our thought processes is what gets us into trouble; we automatically want to talk ourselves out of our feelings, like we would with an illogical thought. But this also halts the emotion. Thoughts can be proven right or wrong, but emotions can't. Like the chair in the room, emotions are energetic entities that do exist. So, just like you would never say that chair shouldn't be there, because it's there, from the same logic you can never say that an emotion shouldn't be there, because it's also there.

As we discussed earlier, for an emotion to be processed and, therefore, disappear, the emotion must be seen, validated, and accepted.

Before my ah-ha moment, I understood the emotional loop of expression as the vehicle to process trauma and past scars, but this experience took my understanding to a deeper, more applicable level. When I started to allow the true emotions under the surface to be there, thereby applying the principle of heard/seen and validated in the moment, I simultaneously witnessed the operationalized response from my ego to hide, fade, or fix the emotion. Since I became aware of it, it then equipped me with the ability to undo this response (which was a fascinating experience to witness). The awareness provided a deep insight into the life of emotions. After this 'ah-ha' moment, I created a ton of space inside myself and allowed the primary feeling of bothered to be there and I told myself, "Of course, this bothers you; it was a very unpleasant experience and even though I am a therapist and feel like I should be 'beyond' being bothered about petty stuff, I am still human . . . so it's okay to feel this." This whole dialogue with my bothered feelings and my reactions to it took myself through several stages of the emotional loop, resulting in the allowance and the surrender of the emotion. What was fascinating is that within days, the potency of that "bothered" feeling almost vanished. I was allowing the truth of my experience to be there, I let myself go to what I was feeling, and then I created space for it, which is really accepting it.

Ultimately emotions aren't a problem to be solved but a wave to be ridden.

That day, I learned another technique for riding my emotional waves. I learned that when you see, validate, and accept your emotions, they move! A lot of people feel stuck in life, and I think it's because they don't know how to release their emotions and are likely afraid to go in and feel them again. The irony is that by feeling your emotions and accepting them, they leave, and you get to feel that lightening of emotional energy, which equates to liberation.

This process really echoes what many spiritual traditions have said with the phrase "the truth will set you free." If we can look at our emotional reactions to events and experiences as they are, we are completely confronting what is. In that confrontation, we are allowing the truth to set us free, and I also think we are coming from a place of openness and love, as opposed to defensiveness and fear.

> *"To heal is to touch with love that which we previously touched with fear."*
> — Stephen Levine

We want to get to a place where we allow ourselves to feel what we need to feel, and we simultaneously accept what happened to us and our feelings about what happened to us. Again, it's not an intellectual exercise—we must connect with the emotions and allow them to move through us, and how we do that will vary person to person.

Going back to the analogy of emotions being like waves in the ocean, I think emotional healing is highly equivalent to surfing. How you ride your own emotional current will be unique to you, and this book is about helping you figure out how not to be afraid of the water, how to connect with your own emotional waves, and, ultimately, how to surf. We will learn not to fight the wave either, because just like the ocean, if you fight the emotional current inside of you, you will be pummeled.

With time and experience, we come to learn that emotions want to move and the only way to release them is by allowing and creating space for that movement to happen. What you will discover when you reach a place of acceptance and emotional honesty is that with each experience, you will feel more and more free. As much as you might think going back and looking at your traumas will be painful and terrifying, the reality is that while it will be difficult, you already experienced the worst part of it—the experience itself. And, by being willing to look at your past, you can release the repressed energy associated with your past, and then it can no longer hurt or haunt you.

Another thing to know is that the emotions themselves feel so painful and/or intense because they have been repressed, and likely repressed with a slew of other emotions, which only intensifies the feeling of emotional overwhelm. Because of this our triggers and acting out behaviors can feel so out of control. In fact, many clients have reported feeling like a monster takes over in the moments when they are triggered. They say things and do things they feel horribly about later. This is truly because repressed emotional energy when stuffed deep down inside will seek ways out and sometimes those ways will feel aggressive. Because the emotions have been held down, they are violently seeking ways to let off steam—like the boiling pot of water analogy, the lid comes flying off.

> "Unexpressed emotions will never die. They are
> buried alive and will come forth
> later in uglier ways."
> — Freud.

Know that the aggressiveness and the ugliness only speak to the lack of awareness of your emotional scars and the more you go within and increase your emotional awareness, the more you will be able to make contact with your repressed emotional energy and the more you can release your repressed emotions in healthy, conscious ways. And once you start releasing that energy, the intensity and the pressure will also lessen, and with each layer you shed, you will feel lighter and more connected to yourself quite simply because emotional repression and stored energy blocks us from ourselves. Imagine, if you will, all that repressed energy being represented by bricks in our body. Once you remove a brick, the whole system can reunite so that with each healing episode, you become more connected, whole, and more you.

Now, as we remember the events that happened and our feelings about it, we may even experience our true emotional reactions to these events for the first time. Repression dictated that a lot, if not all, of those emotions got filed away outside of our awareness—like in the above example with the loss of a dog, you might not even consciously know you were upset your mom wasn't there. That's why remembering all aspects of our trauma is vital for healing these incomplete emotional loops, because we likely will discover things that we had no idea upset us. And once we do this, we are on our way toward completing those emotional loops and healing our past emotional scars. Once you learn how to access and express your emotions and start to clear out the leftover emotional clutter, you will eventually build a more solid foundation where you are more connected to yourself. There is nothing that beats the feeling of being centered and grounded and at peace with your past experiences and being able to accept and live your emotional truth.

Exercises

In the next exercise, you are going to explore what your emotional truth is by thinking of a situation that still triggers you. I want you to write about the situation and then write about your emotional reaction to your emotions. Then ask yourself, what happens if I take the top emotions (the reaction to the emotions) off and allow the truth of my emotions to remain?

_____

_____

_____

_____

CHAPTER 3
Healing Trauma

How do we heal from trauma?

So, this is the deal with trauma, when we experience a difficult life event, we naturally cut off our emotions because we must attend to the trauma, and therefore all other functions, aside from the fight, flight, or freeze, are turned off.

In trauma, emotions are halted from being experienced. In fact, many times, we don't even achieve Step 2 of the emotional loop hierarchy (feeling our emotions with the body) because repression happens instinctually and unconsciously with the body; it clenches and holds in the emotion to attend to the environmental threat, preventing any emotional movement from occurring. This is why survivors of trauma commonly express feeling outside of themselves when the trauma happened—because of the potency of the experience, they had to disconnect from their "felt sense" experience of it. Since it was necessary to survive the moment through activating the reptilian brain thereby repressing their feelings in response to the trauma, they naturally disconnected from the somatic sensations tied to their emotional reaction. This makes a ton of sense because it is the body that houses our emotional experience, and it is with the body that we feel and express our emotions. If we need to not feel, then it follows that we will also have to disconnect from our somatic experience to a certain degree. From here those emotions become trapped in the body and likely are held within the muscular skeletal system itself. What we then must do is become skilled at not noticing any of that pent up tension inside of us. This *not noticing* turns into an utter lack of awareness or denial of those areas—we become unconscious of the material and this operationalized process in the body successfully leads to emotional repression.

"When psychologists are referring to the uncon-
scious, it is the body that
they are talking about."
— Author Unknown

Now, since the way we survived our trauma moments was by holding in our emotions, it only follows that the way we continue to survive is by continuing to keep emotional repression cut off from our awareness. We literally have no idea what is repressed, that's a condition of repression—to be unconscious of it. This works for a while until perhaps our psyche feels safe enough or our environment feels stable enough (or perhaps a mixture of both) to demand that we reconcile this halting and compartmentaliza-tion of a large part of our experience. This coupled with the fact that we are likely experiencing some symptoms (anxiety, depression, OCD, temper tantrums, somatic symptoms, or triggers) or have developed some form of addiction (codependency, alcoholism, binge eating, shopping, watching too much TV, or playing video games, etc.). All the above symptoms and addictions will eventually become overwhelming which will likely beg our psyche to heal and do what we must to reclaim the lost energetic parts of ourselves. This is why I now view any symptom—be it anxiety, triggers, addictions or pangs of depression—as messengers and I welcome the information they carry, because they are here to tell us what we need to do to feel and be whole, authentic, and more connected.

If we follow these symptoms to the essence of what's underneath them, we arrive at our emotional truth. Working through trauma will help you get to a point where you see your emotions or mental health symptoms as allies and not something to be squelched or eradicated. The way we start the process of making friends with and healing our emotions is to do the opposite of what we did to disconnect from them—now instead of ignor-ing them or forgetting them, we simply start to remember. And we first begin this process by remembering our past which will likely lead us to remember the pain we've been carrying associated with our past.

We survived by forgetting, now we heal by remembering.

"Those pains you feel are messengers.
Listen to them."
— Rumi

Trauma-focused cognitive behavioral therapy (TF-CBT) is one of the most effective treatment modalities utilized in working with trauma. I see the underpinning of this approach as really mirroring the process of exposure therapy for phobias. Let me explain.

When we develop a phobia, we have a natural reaction of avoidance. Be it spiders or heights or water—when we are phobic of something, we want to avoid it. Now, if you came into my office and told me about your phobia of snakes, and I decided to implement the best practice for "curing" a phobia such as yours, I would implement a modality that harnesses exposure therapy. What this means is that I would have you expose yourself to snakes in a little-by-little way in a safe and even relaxing environment. First, I would have you think about snakes, and then maybe I would have you look at a picture of a snake, then a video, and then maybe see a snake in a tank at a shop from a distance, and so on. We would slowly have you expose yourself to this stimulus so you would get so used to it, the avoidance response would be dismantled, and the anxiety associated with the phobia would become lessened because nothing bad happened during any of your exposure experiences. You would learn that this stimulus is not really anything to be afraid of through numerous experiences that showed a safe outcome. This is the same thing we do when treating trauma.

Similar to a phobia, what happens when we experience a trauma is we file it away unconsciously, and then we develop an intense propensity to not bring the memory to the forefront of our mind—we avoid looking at it, talking about it, or thinking about it at all costs. In fact, most people coming out of trauma experiences completely avoid anything having to do with their trauma, just like you would a phobia. It's like they figurately put it in a box and file it away deep inside their psyche, and then they avoid any mention or thought related to it. Again, this is right in line with repression. Now, for some, what happens after a trauma is the memories of the trauma break forth time and again in the form of flashbacks or nightmares, which activate fear and anxiety. This phenomenon really highlights that all the trapped emotions associated with the trauma are still inside and the flashbacks and nightmares are happening because the pressure of that emotional repression is seeking ways to let off steam to lessen the pressure. Over time the trauma survivor's response of repression/avoidance will result in increasing mental health symptoms which will continue to communicate that there is healing to be done.

So once their psyche is 'ready' to heal, a modality like TF-CBT can help them figuratively take that box out of the corners of their mind and open it and then with time, support, and the implementation of soothing techniques they will look at the contents from every angle imaginable so they can start to release some of the repressed energy. While they are releasing the repressed energy, they are also exposing themselves to their trauma memory over and over again, and this exposure results in them getting used to their trauma memory; in this way they expose themselves to it so it's no longer this jolting thing that creates fear. Instead, they habituate to it on some level by looking at it, remembering it, feeling the feelings associated with it, and then eventually, they learn it can't hurt them anymore. What then happens is they realize that they have survived it and that they are stronger than it. Remembering your story starts to bring a sense of strength and vindication. You realize how amazing it is that you got through this.

Like I said before I think one of the final stages is realizing that your trauma may have a purpose in this world. When you realize that maybe you can help other people through a similar experience somehow, whether it's getting to be there for someone processing a comparable trauma or serving the community by educating the specifics around your trauma, it changes the way you view what's happened to you. Who knows what it is but thinking that maybe our pain is not in vain and that maybe we can help others *because* of our experience really takes our healing to the next level. As Brené Brown said, "One day you will tell your story of how you overcame what you went through, and it will become someone else's survival guide."

Once our story is something to be proud of, the need to avoid the memory is gone and the trauma can then be integrated. And because nothing bad happened by remembering and processing the emotions around the trauma, and in fact a sense of purpose and inspiration was experienced, the neural pathway that linked the trauma to the reptilian brain becomes lessened and a new neural pathway that links the trauma to the higher brain is formed.

The more we process the trauma the more relief we experience and the more our symptoms fade as well, just like what would happen with recovering from a phobia. This is how successful trauma treatment works, and I have had the honor of witnessing dozens of clients arrive at this "end" point.

For some of you, maybe your history doesn't have extreme traumas, but for others, maybe it does. I will mention again to ensure safety that if you haven't processed your traumas before, you should do this while working with a licensed therapist. But if you have already done the work or you don't have severe traumas, the exercises below can aid in this process.

Healing exercises

I'm going to list several exercises below. After the first two questions, it will be a good idea to space out the rest—don't do all of them in one day. I would even recommend doing one a week or even longer in between, just so you have time to process what comes up. Remember healing is a journey, not a check list.

1. Write a little bit about what you think has been locked away. You could catalogue these with a word or sentence if you had more than one. If you have trauma that is difficult to even think about, try pairing this activity with a higher-brain activity (like meditation or accessing humor) before and after to help navigate difficult emotions (if you feel safe doing this on your own):

_____

_____

_____

_____

_____

_____

_____

_____

2. Next, let's talk a little bit about your symptoms: What are they and what repressed energy do you think they might be tied to? Remember when we repress, we do it unconsciously, so you might not have a clear answer, but whatever comes to mind write down:

_____

_____

_____

_____

_____

_____

_____

3. Timeline: Now, let's start to connect with the repressed energy a little more head-on by going more into detail (again pair with HB activities before and after). For your timeline, you are going to write out or video record your life story. You don't have to go into tremendous detail yet; this is an expansion of the catalogue of difficult moments. But this time, you are going to explore your actual story—make it more like a narration without going too deep into past traumas. You can also chunk this down into decades or chapters based on chronology (maybe a lot happened in your youth, so you can space it out a bit). You might want to get a separate journal for this, but I have provided space below in case you can fit it all here:

_____

_____

_____

_____

_____

_____

_____

4. Before we get into specific traumas with detail, remind yourself that life is a classroom, not a fairytale, we are here to learn, grow and to help others do the same. Ask yourself, how can your trauma(s) turn into something

that you can grow from? How can you use your trauma experience(s) to help others? Again when we can make our trauma(s) a gift to help others, we take it to another level of healing. Write down your answer here:

_____

_____

_____

_____

_____

_____

_____

_____

5. Next, ask yourself, how can you turn this into a tool for yourself? What can you take away from this experience in terms of positives about yourself (i.e., how strong I am, how resilient, etc.)? Write down your answers here:

_____

_____

_____

_____

_____

_____

_____

6. Happy place visual: Before diving into more challenging memories and events, let's create a happy place visual. This can serve as an anchor to be used before you delve into past traumas, as well as something to ground you when you are done. Also, I recommend doing this for a couple of days before you move forward into delving into your trauma. To begin this visual, you will start by closing your eyes and focusing on your breath. Alternate ten deep inhales through your nose and ten exhales through your mouth counting: inhale one . . . exhale two. Now, imagine on each inhale, you bring in fresh oxygen, and on the exhale, you release any tension making the exhale longer than the inhale. From here, you will imagine yourself walking down a hallway, making a mental note of what the hallway and floor look like. At

the end of the hallway, you will see a big door- walk toward this door, and as you get closer, you will see in big letters "My Happy Place." Now, open the door, step through the threshold, and take in your happy place. Pay attention to what you see, to any smells or sounds or other sensations you have and become acutely aware of how you feel in your body. Also notice if anyone else is there with you. This ideally should activate your higher brain so you will naturally start feeling more positive emotions—the goal is to help you feel content and at peace when you finish. You might have to do this a few times to get comfortable with it. And don't worry if it's not crystal clear; mine can sometimes be foggy, but I get a sense of it and it always make me feel grounded. Let's have you now do your happy place visual and afterwards write down what happened here:

_____

_____

_____

_____

_____

_____

_____

Trauma visualization exercises

Before you begin your trauma visualization exercises, in preparation for an emotional release, make sure to have soothing tools on standby (candles, music, warm fuzzy blankets, or a cup of tea, etc.). Now is the time to nurture yourself. And, after your emotional release, to reground yourself, do your happy place visual again.

1. Visualize your trauma event happening in chronological order while pairing it with your happy place visual—doing it before and after (remember to do one difficult event at a time with at least a few days in between and consider starting with the mildest first). Again, if it's highly traumatic to even think about, do this with a coach or therapist. As you visualize, focus on connecting with the thoughts and feelings that were present during the trauma: What did you tell yourself before, during, and after? What did you

feel before, during, and after? You might not remember some or even all your thoughts and feelings, and that's okay. They have been repressed—this exercise is about you starting to remember. So, even if a little memory comes up, you are doing it "right." If a lot of emotion comes out, that's okay, too—that's really what we are aiming for.

Now, let's have you do your trauma visualization. Write down what happened here or in your journal:

_____

_____

_____

_____

_____

_____

_____

_____

"Healing begins the moment you accept the hurt."
— Sonia Motwani

2. Changing history: This exercise is rooted in the idea that during times of trauma or difficult life experiences, we have unfulfilled experiences and/or unmet needs. For example, maybe we really needed to feel supported when our best friend dumped us for another friend, but nobody was available to do that, or when your dad was yelling and screaming, you really need to feel like someone was going to save you or stick up for you. This exercise helps to fulfill unmet needs through imaging that you got the need fulfilled way back when. You may ask, how on earth does this help anything? You may even be wondering if it might make it worse because it's highlighting what didn't happen. Well, all I can tell you is that the brain can't tell the difference between a visual or a real-life experience, and imagining it literally creates a new neural pathway as if it really happened, which I believe loosens the hold of our trauma neural pathways. And if you can

relive it in your mind, it will feel like it happened on some level, and at the very least, it will cure the desire for that need. I have done this exercise with myself, as well as with dozens of clients, and I will say it has always provided some type of shift, be it small or monumental. At the very least, it's worth exploring.

Start out with your happy place visual and then go back into one of your trauma moments, but this time, let your trauma have an alternate ending—imagine someone coming in to save you. It could be an aunt or famous person you admire or even your older self: What would you have liked to have happen? How would you have wanted it resolved? Note: You can do this repeatedly. The more you expose yourself to your trauma, the more habituated you become to the trauma feelings and the more it will start to be integrated. Write down what happened here:

_____

_____

_____

_____

_____

_____

_____

"When we deny the story, it defines us. When we own the story, we can write a brave new ending."
— Brené Brown

3. Younger-self exercise: The next exercise is tied to John Bradshaw's inner-child work (John Bradshaw, Homecoming, 1990), which is, hands down, my favorite intervention—not only as a technique I use with my clients, but one that I did during my own personal therapeutic work. The purpose of this technique is to connect with the younger versions of you in order to rescue and integrate them into who you are now. What happens is that whenever we experience a trauma or have unmet needs, we become emotionally arrested at whatever age it occurred.

The developmental arrest happens for a couple different reasons. One, when we experience a trauma, the energy around our emotional reaction becomes repressed, resulting in parts of us becoming stuck. So, if you had a trauma at age five, ten, and fourteen, for example, you now have a stuck five-, ten-, and fourteen-year-old inside you, or at least, you have the leftover feelings from that time that are linked to that younger version. And two, many of us likely weren't given the support to navigate our development, which also creates many unfulfilled needs and repressed emotions at certain ages. In both circumstances, we disconnect from that version of ourselves, and it prevents us from being able to be a whole and authentic individual later in life. As the goal of healing is really wholeness and authenticity, we must reclaim all pieces of ourselves to truly move closer toward that goal.

Also, they say that an element of healthy emotional development and healing is when we learn to become our own parent; this is when we can finally give the younger versions of us exactly what they needed in terms of love and support. With this technique, you get to experience what it feels like to have your inner child's needs meet emotionally. For those of you who struggle with self-esteem and regard yourself poorly, this will likely help, because when you look at yourself as an innocent child, how can you not start to have more self-compassion? For me personally, after doing inner-child work, for the first time in my life, I understood what it felt like to really love myself. When I think about the little girl in me, how perfect and filled with goodness she was/is, how can I not love her? And loving her is loving me, which is healing in and of itself.

Younger-self Exercise:

To begin this exercise, we will do a similar introduction as we did for the Happy Place Visual. You will get comfortable and start to focus on your breath. Alternate ten deep inhales through your nose and ten exhales through your mouth counting: inhale one . . . exhale two. Now, imagine on each inhale, you bring in fresh oxygen, and on the exhale, you release any tension making the exhale longer than the inhale. From here, you will imagine yourself walking down a hallway to a big door. Once you get to the door, you will see engraved with big letters, "My Younger-Self." Once you open the door, you will find yourself in a room with two chairs facing each other; sit in one of those chairs. Then imagine the younger version of you coming in and sitting across from you; engage them in conversation. Ask them (and really see them as separate) what it's like for them in their life, what they need for support, what did they need and not get, and then ask them anything else that comes to mind. Wait patiently as they answer. Now is your chance to become the person that they needed at that time by telling them everything they needed to hear. Tell them it was never their fault, they did nothing wrong, they are perfect just as they are—whatever else would resonate for them (or the younger you). If it feels organic, maybe even see yourself scooping them up and hugging them. Ideally, emotions flow with this exercise, but if for some reason it's hard to get into it the first time, try it again after a few days. The more you go in, usually the easier it is to connect. If it is successful, know that you can do this for each age or moment in time you may be stuck, and you can repeat this exercise as much as you like. Use the space below to record your experience:

_____

_____

_____

_____

_____

_____

_____

_____

4. Letter writing to yourself exercise: If there is a lot of anger or resentment toward yourself that manifests from your exploration—like maybe you blame yourself for a decision you made in your past—you can write a letter of forgiveness to the younger version of you. What could be helpful to aid in this is to think of other people you know who are around the same age as you were when you made your mistake. Ask yourself, would they be responsible if something similar happened to them? Also ask yourself if you would be harsh or critical toward them for the decisions they might make? Think of the younger version of yourself here, too. Would you be mad at a sixteen-year-old for making a bad decision? Remind yourself that

most of the time bad decisions are what help us learn what good decisions are, and they hold the potential for growth.

_____

_____

_____

_____

_____

_____

_____

5. Narrative therapy exercise: Imagine your life is a movie: What role do the people in your life play? Who is the villain? What role do you play (hero/heroine)? Who are the supporting actors? What is the theme of your movie? What would the title be? What are some good endings? What's it like to see your life from a broader lens? This exercise is really great with aiding in perspective! Remember, perspective is a function of the higher brain, and looking at our past through this lens can aid in loosening the RB's hold on our past scars, as well as potentially giving us more information we may not have seen before. Write your answers below:

_____

_____

_____

_____

_____

_____

_____

_____

6. Letter writing others exercise: From doing your timeline, conflict with others likely surfaced. Maybe your caregivers weren't there in the way you needed or a past romantic partner betrayed you. A way to start to access and process the feelings around these relationships is through writing a letter. This is where you write a letter to your past people to express repressed emotions authentically. The authenticity piece is vital, which is why you will be

writing with the intention of NOT SENDING the letter. You want to write without worrying about editing; you just want to get it out and you want to be honest with how you feel. You might be thinking, "But wait, I know so-and-so meant well; they didn't mean to (fill in the blank), and I've already forgiven them." Again, one of the biggest and most common mistakes we make with our feelings is by assuming that if our minds have accepted historic experiences, moved on, and forgiven whoever did what, then our feelings have followed suit. This is false—if you haven't cried and gotten angry with whomever over whatever, you likely haven't released the repressed emotions.

Remember, emotions aren't supposed to be logical—they are energy that wants to move. You have to create the space for them to do that without moving to hide, fade, or fix them. Think of them, again, like a wave in the ocean. The wave isn't right or wrong, and the only thing you can do with the wave is ride it. If you fight it or control it, you will get pummeled. And the irony is that if you feel and accept your emotions, they will in fact move. Also, when we go right to forgiveness in our head without honoring our feelings, we aren't being honest. This, although well intentioned, will keep us stuck with the emotional energy. List below the people you want to write and not send letters to:

1. _____
2. _____
3. _____
4. _____
5. _____
6. _____
7. _____
8. _____

And now start with the first person on your list:

DEAR:_____

_____
_____
_____
_____
_____

_____

_____

_____

_____

_____

Triggers are messengers, and we can follow them to heal

Okay, here is the interesting part- often, we might not know what we have repressed inside of us. After all, that is the whole point of repression— to *forget* and literally not know what we have emotionally cut off. Many people come to my office knowing they have stuff likely trapped inside of them because of their symptoms but have no clue what that stuff really is and have no idea how to access it. This is the brilliant piece of the human condition; we can learn what is stuck inside of us by looking at our reactions to things that happen on the outside of us.

This is where a trigger or flooding or being emotionally activated (all terms describing the same thing) comes in. Your triggers will tell you a ton about what you need to heal and process. Like we talked about before, our triggers are more about the past than the present. If you are wondering how to tell if your reaction is truly a trigger, and therefore rooted in the past, ask yourself if your present emotional reaction is out of proportion to what is happening currently. If your reaction is way bigger than the situation warrants, then you are likely battling ghosts from yesterday. I always tell my clients, when we get triggered, it's like we pulled out an old move projector and we are now watching a scene from our past transposed on our current relationships. It's so important to identify if you are triggered, because it will be vital to unplug from the now and go explore the emotions from the past (we will discuss this in more depth in the coming chapter on relationship conflicts).

"Every time you are triggered, it is a sign that you must go deep and heal yourself with love."
— Author Unknown

Trigger exercises

Now, let's explore what triggers you experience by doing some exercises.
1. Who triggers you? Once this is identified, ask yourself, who do they remind you of or what does your relationship's dynamic activate inside of you? Find the time, relationship, or event in your past that this pulls on. Once you have identified that, look at your specific feelings or thoughts about yourself and the world because of this moment. Ask yourself, what did I tell myself about this event? What did I tell myself about myself? What decision did I make about the world? What decisions did I make about how I would behave moving forward because of this? This is vital to uncover because often these decisions keep us stuck by creating automatic thoughts and core beliefs that tend to be distorted and are therefore false. Write your discoveries below:

_____

_____

_____

_____

_____

_____

_____

_____

One thing to note is that just because you are having an emotional reaction to something going on in your world doesn't always mean it's a trigger from the past. Sometimes our emotions rear their heads in order for us to pay attention and respond accordingly.

Emotions are messengers too

As much as we think our emotions are our enemies, or they are out of control and need to be reined in, the reality is that they carry very important information. They tell you how you are experiencing the given moment and may indicate what needs to be healed or what action needs to be enacted. Again, think of the emotion anger. Often anger communicates that a boundary has been violated and the anger that emerges is trying to propel you to set an immediate boundary. The anger is there to help you do this. If you listen to this feeling and you set a boundary, you will be taking care of yourself. Anger can also become a secondary emotion, where it is trying to protect softer emotions, like fear or sadness. In both instances, anger is a messenger. If we go inward and follow our emotions to the root, we can discover our emotional truth for what has happened in the past as well as how we are feeling about what is happening now.

By being connected to our feelings and expressing our feelings, we remain in touch with ourselves, so when we listen to what we really need and act on it, we won't lose ourselves. Often, once we cut off our emotions from our awareness, we start to not really know ourselves anymore. If we stop listening to ourselves, we will be out of touch with our true self. This happens a lot with traditional females- when they are in a romantic relationship, they tend to merge themselves with the other and become accommodating. If we become too agreeable and focus only on pleasing the other, we stop focusing on ourselves and what we want. What results eventually is that we have no idea what we feel, want, or who we even are. It would be like if we all a sudden, stopped calling or having gatherings with a friend—once enough time passes, we would feel like we don't know that person anymore. It's the same thing with ourselves if we stop hearing and expressing what we are feeling. And if we don't really know who we are, how on earth can we share ourselves with other people? We can't. So when we lose ourselves, we also lose the ability to be truly intimate. The way we connect with others is by sharing our truth, and if we don't know what it is, we hardly can do that.

One of the ways to stay connected to ourselves is by listening to and exploring our feelings about things and allowing whatever comes up to come up and truly being okay with that. We so often talk ourselves out of our emotions, which isn't helpful, but if we remember that feelings just need to be expressed, heard/seen, and validated and they aren't right or wrong, we will be able to learn how to manage our emotional experiences.

Remember, if we allow them to be there and come to accept them, they will move. Also remember that intense emotions could be a reflection of repressed energy, the intensity communicating that there is healing that needs to happen. While other times intense emotions may be messengers for what we are experiencing in the here and now and what we need to do about it. Taking both of these scenarios into account, our emotions provide information, whether it's about what skill sets need to be developed (effective communication, coping strategies, or conflict resolution) or what parts of our past need to be healed.

And if we view emotions in a way that elevates their status from nonsensical and immature to valuable and informative, knowing that emotions are our psyche's way of communicating with us, we can learn to harness the information they bring. Once we integrate our emotions into our present life experience, we then have a good sense of how to take care of ourselves. Then we can become more authentic and able to connect with others—again, the name of the game.

CHAPTER 4
Self-talk, the RB, and Repressed Emotions

Why do we listen to negative self-talk?

Did you know that researchers estimate that we have something like 1,000 thoughts per minute? You might be thinking, "There is no way I have ever experienced that many thoughts bombarding my mind." Even if you are aware of the mental chatter, you likely aren't aware of the content of those thoughts. Especially because many of them—maybe even 980 of them— are subconscious or even unconscious. And if you turn inward and focus on your self-talk what you will notice is that some of these thoughts are "positive" and some are "negative." And depending on the day and what is going on in your world one might rule more than the other.

> *"It's not what you say out of your mouth that deter-*
> *mines your life, it's what you whisper to yourself*
> *that has the most power."*
> - Robert T. Kiyosaki

I have come to think of these "positive" and "negative" thoughts from the nostalgic childhood lens of the angel and devil on your shoulder. The angel speaks of hope, encouragement, perspective, silver linings, all your strengths and accomplishments, and reframes others' behaviors in a positive light, whereas the devil speaks of how bad things are, how bad you are, how bad people are, worst-case scenarios, and fear-laden warnings. The angel says things to you like, "You can do it," or "Well, at least you learned (fill in the blank) from this experience," or "So-and-so is just grouchy, don't take it personally," and so on. But the devil says things like, "You are a horrible person," or "You will never be good enough," or "Nobody likes you," or "It's all your fault so-and-so is mean to you," or "You can't trust anyone," and so on. What I have come to understand about this dualistic experience happening below our awareness is that both voices are there, and both seem to be credible when they are listened to. But the validity of both is not equal. To illustrate this, let's explore our neuroanatomy when placed within the context of negative versus positive self-talk.

When the angel or the devil is dominating, which part of the brain do you think is being utilized respectively? If you're not sure, ask yourself how you feel when the positive thoughts are flowing through your mind and then think about how it feels when the negative thoughts kick in. You will likely say that the angel brings with it feelings of hope and inspiration, whereas the devil elicits feelings of hopelessness or fear. Along these lines, knowing what we already know about the brain, we can discern that the higher brain is activated with positive self-talk and the lower brain is activated with negative self-talk. From here, we can deduce which voice is truly more accurate—going back to one simple fact that the higher brain holds more gray matter than the lower brain. So, knowing the devil has less brain power and occupies maybe 2% of the brain, how accurate do you think its thoughts are? Nowhere near accurate! This also means that the thoughts that come from the figurative angel are going to be closer to truth, because quite simply, the higher brain has access to problem solving, big picture thinking, logic, and perspective. We know this part of the brain has access to what is true, whereas the devil's side does not.

Then, why does the negative thoughts feel so accurate when they're speaking? There are a few different reasons. First, because negative self-talk resides in the reptilian brain and this part of the brain functions from a fight/flight/freeze place. Thoughts that come from the RB place will naturally feel urgent and life or death. This part of the brain when activated naturally puts us into a tailspin because, on some level, we feel like we are in physical danger. From this stance, one reason the devil or the RB comes to speak louder and feel more potent is because it uses fear to get our attention.

Second, the RB can trick us into thinking its voice is truth, because it pulls on our past scars and insecurities. It knows us on a very deep level and therefore uses our past to filter through the negative commentary. So, suddenly, a relatively "benign" self-talk assertion feels like an accurate character assassination. Take, for example, a self-talk statement such as, "You don't matter" -not the nicest thing to hear but could be dismissed just as a fleeting negative thought. However, when heard by someone who felt like they didn't matter in childhood, it suddenly evokes a more intense reaction. For this particular person, this self-talk statement is highly triggering because it hits on past experiences when they already felt like they didn't matter and, therefore, reaffirms their already long-held belief. When this happens, we feel like these thoughts must be true because the negative thoughts are echoing thoughts we had way back when. In fact, deeply rooted thoughts that we hold onto and that come to influence how we are in the world turn into automatic (i.e., unconscious) beliefs. And what has been discovered in psychology is that once an automatic belief is established, it becomes very difficult to undo. In the context of negative self-talk, I have found that it is our long held automatic beliefs that come to be at the root of a lot of our triggers, and the material the devil will come to pull on, later in life. Let's explore the phenomena of long-held automatic beliefs more in depth, which will bring us to a discussion on *automatic core beliefs* (ACBs).

What happens when we go through a trauma is that we tell ourselves something about ourselves and the world. In the example above the person likely told themselves something like, "People don't pay attention to me (or fill in the blanks), because I must not matter." From this statement comes the belief that I don't matter, which feels true, and over time, it becomes solidified into an automatic core belief.

An automatic core belief (ACB) is a concept that describes how an unconscious belief is held deep inside without awareness and will come to influence how the individual shows up in the world, how they respond to others, and how they think of themselves inherently. It becomes a story they tell themselves about themselves, other people, and the world, and unfortunately, many of these beliefs, when created in response to difficult life events, become negative in nature and become the material that ignites our triggers in our present life. So, if the "devil" uses an ACB, of course we are going to pay more attention because it's essentially using our triggers and past wounds to get our attention even though these assertions are likely not true. Again, the RB is maybe 2% of our brain. It was designed to *act* not *think* so, of course, the thoughts it produces that don't pertain to immediate survival won't be accurate. Most of what it says will be illusions, distortions, and lies.

Once we know the RB's strategies to keep our attention, we have to appreciate that while the reptilian brain is vital for survival, it is toxic when used for any other purpose. Therefore, being able to interrupt the RB from taking over and ruling our mind is key. And while learning when the RB/devil is talking is the first step in doing something about it, the next step is just as vital, to keep it from dominating.

This next step involves learning how not to give this part of the brain anymore strength than it deserves. You might ask, how do we give it strength thereby learning how not to give it strength? The fable "The Two Wolves" below illustrates the "how" for both very succinctly:

An old Cherokee is teaching his grandson about life. "A fight is going on inside me," he said to the boy. "It is a terrible fight and it is between two wolves. One is evil—he is anger, envy, sorrow, regret, greed, arrogance, self-pity, guilt, resentment, inferiority, lies, false pride, superiority, and ego." He continued, "The other is good—he is joy, peace, love, hope, serenity, humility, kindness, benevolence, empathy, generosity, truth, compassion, and faith. The same fight is going on inside you—and inside every other person, too."

The grandson thought about it for a minute and then asked his grandfather, "Which wolf will win?"

The old Cherokee simply replied, "The one you feed."

After doing therapy with others for almost two decades and working with more than thirty clients weekly, I have come to understand self-talk on a deeper level. Over the years, I have seen that the pull of the RB from the HB is incredibly potent and palpable; you can literally see it take place while talking to someone who is triggered or who lives in their lower brain. That pull feels like it wants to keep individuals away from their higher-brain thoughts, and it's almost like separate entities are forever at battle, just like the fable names. Again it's just like what my daughter said about the reptilian brain when she was young, "Mama, I'm getting good at knowing when I'm in the RB, but when I'm there, I don't want to get out." The reality is that it becomes strong from use, and like the fable above delineates—if we feed it, it will rule us—and we will come to believe what it tells us. This, unfortunately, includes telling us that the RB thoughts are real. Once we believe its voice to be true, we will not only not see a way out, but we will believe there is no reason to get out. Or better yet, we won't think there is any 'out' to get out from since the RB *is* reality.

> *"The only lies for which we are truly punished are those we tell ourselves."*
> — V. S. Naipaul

What do you think the equivalent of feeding it is when it comes to negative versus positive self-talk? We feed it by listening to it, believing it, and giving it our attention. If we focus on it and get sucked into its thoughts, because the brain is a muscle, this part of the brain naturally will become stronger and stronger. And once it's strong enough, it will dominate to the point where we will start to live there. At this point, we will naturally come to believe the lies it tells us, because this is our only reality. So, the question then becomes: What can we do about it?

The answer to this question is twofold:

- heal repressed emotions
- build higher-brain neural pathways

We know the RB's potency is from our trauma history, so if we start to heal our neural pathway 'scar tissue' and we correct the distorted thoughts that go along with that scar tissue, the self-talk that tries to hook into those cognitive distortions won't work. Let's use the example again with the phrase "You don't matter", when spoken to someone who felt like they didn't matter in childhood. If they can go back and heal the wounds associated with that thought, they can correct that automatic belief and come to see that it is and was always a lie. They will learn that not being good enough was never true. This person will then need to release all the emotions, or a fair number of emotions, related to their core experiences that solidified this ACB. What will then happen is the intensity around that thought will dissolve and the "devil" will not have a leg to stand on.

We won't believe that thought anymore or any of the negative self-talk that is tied to it when the emotional energy that gave it power has been healed and released. And if we can do this with all or most of our automatic beliefs, we can truly feed the voice that hooks into our truth. Then it will be easy to see through the RB's pull to bring us down. Remember the reality is the angel is stronger by nature—it holds way more gray matter than the RB. It's always been an illusion that our negative self-talk is accurate.

Once we start to heal our past wounds, we then need to feed the positive self-talk to build the muscle of the higher brain (and solidify those neural pathways). And again, the most vital first step toward this end is to become good at knowing which part of the brain you are in.

What is the best way to know if you are listening more to the negative self-talk than the positive? Pay attention to how you feel. If you feel down or yucky about yourself or the world and it's not tied to a current situation or, it's out of proportion to the situation, the devil is ruling your self-talk and you are living in your reptilian brain. Again, our feelings are our friends. They are messengers telling us things and this includes shinning a light on what self-talk is occurring in our mind, so we need to pay attention to our feelings because most of the time, we might not even know the RB has taken over- it happens that quickly.

I had this experience a few years ago. I was driving down the road feeling pretty good, in my higher brain, and then all of a sudden, I felt a pit in my stomach. I noticed the shift and immediately started examining what thought it was tied to. It took a few moments, but I was able to get in touch with a sense of shame or feeling like I had done something wrong. I then looked to my thoughts and realized that this feeling was being activated by the recollection of an event I had two years before with a supervisor where I disagreed with his management style on "punishing" staff for not meeting their productivity numbers. Well, I left that meeting feeling bad for confronting him, which completely hit on childhood experiences and an automatic belief that said I always needed to please others, avoid conflict, and not rock the boat. What was fascinating is that this was a fleeting memory that would have been long gone, leaving only negative feelings that felt real, had I not followed my feelings to the root of what instigated it. Once I realized this, I shifted my focus to pleasurable thoughts and did my "I love list" and I was immediately back to my feel-good state of being. It was as easy as that.

In this scenario, I could shift my focus back to higher-brain thoughts because this incident was relatively benign. It wasn't a trauma and I had already done quite a bit of work on correcting my automatic belief that I need to be a "pleaser," so shifting to higher brain was accessible. Now had that not been the case, in terms of healing and correcting that belief, or if the thought was pulling on a more significant memory or trauma, it may have required me to process some of the emotions around the event before I could get back to my HB. Let's look at an example of this.

I had a highly traumatic event involving a group of women. Essentially what happened was a couple of them turned on me, which resulted in them turning others against me as well. This situation happened when I was seventeen, and it really shook me, because I was also grieving the loss of a very dear person in my life at the time. Actually, one of the reasons they turned on me was because they felt like I was crying too much and they were sick of hearing it. I must say, in retrospect, I have compassion for any seventeen-year-old trying to navigate life and I also believe we are all here learning and growing from each other and the most negative encounters are our greatest teachers. But this incident still fostered a very strong ACB when it came to trusting others, especially a group of women, and a part of my ACB told me I should avoid trusting groups of women at all costs. So, after decades went by, I remained unscathed by other women through keeping my distance. In fact, I only really let a few women in, women who I learned I could trust.

Almost thirty years later, I found myself working amongst a circle of women. There ended up being some issues with stability in our employment and some of the women became a bit nervous about their standing. I wanted to help and put myself out there more than I usually do and ended up getting burned. Afterwards, I confronted the individual whom I felt turned on me and gave them a piece of my mind, which was not an available response to me at seventeen (being the pleaser back then).

But that didn't go well, to say the least. Predictably, it exploded and the whole one-woman-turning-many-women-against-me fear manifested right before my eyes. As you can imagine, my negative self-talk had a field day with all of this. The devil on my shoulder became ten feet tall, and all I could hear was that everyone hated me and that I was a horrible, no-good person. Yuck!

Funnily enough, even though I teach this stuff daily, when it happened, it really hit me between the eyes. It's a reminder that everyone on the planet is learning and growing. After this happened, it took a while to get my bearings, because I was overcome with disbelief that this should even affect me, and more succinctly my emotional reaction to the present situation unearthed the emotional residue from the trauma from when I was 17. What intensified the experience was also the phenomena of many in my community not hearing or validating my perspective, which led to the feelings of being gaslit all over again as well, which was predictable. I say predictable because it was like my psyche wanted the dynamics to play out as close to the original wound as possible. Back then it was many individuals turning on me while the rest of my peers stood in disbelief of what I was going through, not knowing what to say and not wanting to get involved. So, this current situation nailed that part of my trauma as well. It makes sense why this current dynamic presented itself in just this way, because the more accurate the event is to the original trauma, the more repressed emotions from that trauma will likely come to the surface—it's like a magnet. And naturally what was vital for me to do with this experience was to see through what was happening in the moment and to recognize that the potency of my emotions as well as my negative self-talk was rooted in my past. It was literally 2% right now, and 98% back then. The scars from the trauma of that seventeen-year-old were still there and were now actively engaged. I felt emotions I hadn't felt in years, and I would probably say I hadn't ever felt, which again signifies that it was successfully repressed. It also indicates that my psyche was now ready to heal deeper layers of this experience.

Once I recognized that this was hardly about a group of women whom I barely knew and was really about healing what I had been through way back when, I actively started implementing healing strategies on myself.

I allowed my emotional loops to be processed through journaling, self-exploration and emotional releases. I also accessed a deeply held unconscious belief (ACB) that said I was to blame for the women turning on me, which led to a correction of that distortion and ultimately forgiving my 17-year-old younger self who was innocent and just needed love and support. After all this work, culminating with correcting my automatic core belief, what followed was a massive 'ah ha!', breakthrough moment and a profound emotional release. After I did this last piece, the potency of the negative thoughts started to subside; the situation held such a strong trigger, but through processing repressed emotions and allowing whatever my emotional reaction was currently to the situation to be there, and correcting my ACB, the trigger became almost non-existent. Unlike the previous example, getting myself to not hook into that negative monologue took time and energy, but once my emotional work lessened the repressed energy and once I was able to unearth and then correct my ACB, it became more doable to implement higher-brain strategies to help me focus on and listen to the angel on my shoulder instead of the devil. And after it was all said and done, I came to feel emotionally lighter as well!

You might ask, why does our psyche wait so long to process an experience? The reality is who knows?! For me, I have been through quite a lot of different traumatic experiences, so I was actually surprised when I realized that I never really explored this one on a deeper level. Perhaps for some people, it's a matter of healing some deeper wounds first before moving toward other ones, while for others, they might just have a few to dive into. I will say, that for both, it does require a certain amount of coping-skill development, along with a sense of psychological safety to be able to do deeper work. Therefore, if you don't feel like you can go there and explore certain memories, don't! Your psyche and your intuition are never wrong.

With that said, I have a few exercises that tie into self-talk exploration and healing below. Feel free to dive in or skip it if it's not what you are needing or a match for where you are emotionally right now.

Self-talk exercises

Let's explore self-talk strategies as they apply to your inner dialogue. When you find yourself feeling not great and you think it's tied to your self-talk, in those moments you can do several things:

- *Explore its roots:* Where does your negative self-talk get its potency from? What automatic belief and past incident is it pulling on?
- *Challenge it:* If your self-talk is fairly benign and not attached to a trauma, challenge your self-talk by asking if it's true what you are telling yourself? Would you talk to a friend in the same way? A ten-year-old?
- *Heal those emotions:* If it is connected to a trauma, retell your trauma story maybe though traditional journaling or even doing a video journal (where you put your phone in front of you, go to the video option and hit 'play'). The emotions are up for a reason—they want to heal. Sometimes, and I might say all the time, we are given the experiences we have to help us do that. As with my own example above, I was not thrilled to be going through girl drama in my forties, but it was the perfect experience to really activate repressed material from my younger years. Maybe this could be the same for you? What is your self-talk triggering?
- *Write a letter:* Write a letter to that younger version of you that decided to believe whatever that negative thought was. Tell them it's not true and was never true. In my example, I needed to realize that just because others are reacting negatively to me, doesn't mean I'm a bad person—it almost always has more to do with them than me. It's important to take responsibility for our part, but also know that this is likely triggering something for the other person(s) as well.
- *Talk to your inner child*: Imagine the older version of you making contact with that younger version to help them heal and to show them that the automatic belief around the negative self-talk is not true.

Let's practice right now:

1. Write down some of your negative self-talk phrases you say often to yourself and then below write about where they come from:

Negative thought:_____
Origins:

_____
_____
_____
_____
_____
_____
_____
_____

Negative thought:_____
Origins:

_____
_____
_____
_____
_____
_____
_____
_____

Negative thought:_____
Origins:

_____
_____
_____
_____
_____
_____
_____

2. For this one, let's challenge the self-talk above and write down what the higher brain (angel) would say to each reptilian brain (Devil) thought(s):

RB/Devil thought_____

HB/Angel thought:_____

RB/Devil thought:_____

HB/Angel thought:_____

RB/Devil thought:_____

HB/Angel thought:_____

3. Next, if you want to do a visual or write a letter to the younger version of you that is tied to the negative self-talk phrases above, you can do that here:

_____

_____

_____

The more practice we get with interrupting negative self-talk and replacing it with higher-brain thoughts, along with healing what needs to heal, the easier it will be to focus on the angel's voice over the devil's. And if we can loosen the figurative scar tissue that binds the lower brain with our amygdala, keeping us stuck in the reptilian brain, we will be able to stay in higher brain all the time. In this way, healing and strengthening the higher brain gives us freedom, so instead of unconsciously reacting to situations internally or externally (which is what the RB does), we can respond consciously (which is what the HB enables us to do). The next chapter will look at all of this—reptilian brain, higher brain, triggers, and self-talk—in the context of romantic relationships, which are arguably the most fertile ground for the RB to rear its ugly or, shall I say, unhealed head!

CHAPTER 5
The RB and Triggers in Romantic Relationships

Do romantic relationships hold the potential to help us heal?

So, I have bad news and good news about romantic relationships. The bad news is romantic relationships almost always bring up our triggers, and the good news is romantic relationships almost always bring up our triggers!

The reason why this is good is because by knowing what our triggers are, we can heal them. Remember our triggers are tied to repressed emotions, and repressed emotions will remain unconscious until we bring them to the surface. Romantic relationships can serve as a magnet for what is blocked and unhealed inside of us, thereby bringing unconscious material to light. Triggers, like mental health symptoms, are a way they come to the surface, so this phenomenon provides very good information about what is going on inside of us. A reason why this is bad news is because triggers have the potential to wreak havoc in relationships. For some, relationships become a battle ground and those in it can experience a sense of anxiety and panic. Often times, many think their triggers are justifiable reactions to what is happening right now when, in reality, their reactions are really rooted in the past.

Let's explore how triggers show up in relationships and what we can do about it.

It happens to all of us. Maybe we are sitting down for dinner and everything is great and then something is said in a certain way and *boom*—we are no longer thinking clearly, our mind races, our blood starts to boil, and we see red. Or maybe your significant other was supposed to text you right after their meeting and you still haven't heard from them. Suddenly, your mind is whirling, and nothing is okay. In these moments, it's like, all of a sudden, the lights are turned off—we no longer have access to clear thinking and our partner, whom we trusted and loved completely a few minutes ago, is suddenly a threat, our enemy, and the source of our fear. These types of experiences describe what it feels like to be emotionally activated or triggered.

The feelings that surface when you are activated emotionally ultimately indicate that you are in your reptilian brain, which means you just lost access to higher-brain thinking (i.e., logic, problem solving, perspective, assessing consequences, etc.) and your lower brain has taken over, telling you that there is danger, and you need to be afraid and suspicious of every-one—especially the person who set off the trigger. So, just like that, your partner suddenly becomes your enemy, and it is kill or be killed on a primal level; fight, flight, or freeze kicks in and you behave accordingly. In this instance you may suddenly accuse your loved one of something, and as a fighter, you begin an interrogation. Or maybe you tend flee, so you shut down and leave the room. Or if you tend to freeze, you might stop engaging all together and even lose touch with yourself in these moments. I've had numerous clients report feeling like they black-out during these times, which isn't far from the truth. The black-out feeling happens because they lose access to a portion of their brain, and once they recover and get out of the RB, it's almost like it didn't happen.

Whatever your mode of responding is, one thing is for certain, you are not thinking clearly or accurately when triggered. To make matters more complicated, because the RB is designed to save your life from physical danger, it is designed to *act*. But, since there is nothing to do in terms of running from a lion or fighting off an assailant, you are left with this urgent I-have-to-do-something energy with nowhere to go. And since it has nowhere to go, all that energy fuels and heightens the intensity of your thoughts. Furthermore, your thoughts are driven to not feel what you are feeling, so they want to, at all costs, eliminate the perceived threat in the moment, whether it is winning the argument with your partner, freezing, and hoping it all stops, or even packing your bags to escape what's happening. The problem with all this is, of course, that you don't have access to the one part of the brain you really need, the part that is good at solving problems and assessing consequences- your higher brain.

This is why we often get into battles in our relationships only to break up or say this or that, and then the next day, when we are back in our higher brain, we ask ourselves, "What the hell happened?!" Suddenly all the conviction from the day before has completely vanished, and you almost can't remember why you got so upset, which means you are out of the reptilian brain and now in your higher brain, thinking more clearly. Knowing all of this, there is only one thing you must do as soon as you get triggered in your relationships. If you learn anything from this chapter at all it is this; when you get activated and you are with your partner and the trigger is toward your partner, you must take a TIME-OUT IMMEDIATELY!

It simply doesn't make sense not to. You don't have access to higher brain thinking, so there is nothing to work out. You will only end up fighting or destroying the relationship. The one caveat is if your partner doesn't get activated, they could help you out of the RB with humor, talking about something you are looking forward to, or some other higher-brain activity—but it might also make it worse. The one thing harder than getting yourself out of your RB is your partner getting you out of your RB, and please don't tell your partner they are in their reptilian brain, that never bodes well either.

Now, if a trigger is unrelated to your relationship, then supporting your partner toward accessing their higher brain might work. This truly is the beautiful part of a partnership: we are here to support each other through the rough moments. You can use humor or maybe distract them with a good movie but know this is not your job. In fact, it really is incumbent upon your partner to get themselves out of the RB, just like it's incumbent upon you to do the same. Ultimately learning how to get out of and navigate our RB is a skill that we all have to get really good at. So, if someone else takes this over for us, we will find ourselves in a codependent situation, where we need our partner to make us feel better, which isn't healthy and eventually will backfire (we will go more into codependency in the next chapter).

To reiterate, when we are triggered in our relationship, we almost always need to institute a time-out to help ourselves out of lower-brain activation. And again, during this time, it is up to each individual to soothe themselves so they can effectively get out of their RB and either get into their HB or process their emotions. Either way, going within is going to provide the necessary information to move forward. Now, usually one person in the relationship has difficulties with taking a time-out, which poses a wrinkle in implementing this strategy consistently. Let's look at why this is by exploring the *pursuer–distancer dynamic*.

What is the pursuer–distancer dynamic?

The pursuer–distancer dynamic—what a cruel joke from the powers that be. What happens with this phenomenon is when both people in the relationship become triggered, one person wants to stay and work through the conflict, and the other one wants to bolt and take a time-out.

The distancer, the one who wants to bolt, gets anxiety if they are forced to stay, and the pursuer, the one who wants to work through the conflict immediately, gets anxiety with parting. From here, what we see is the pursuer pursuing the distancer at all costs and trying to force them to finish the conversation. The distancer predictably is trying to avoid the conversation and likely at this point withdrawing either psychologically or physically or both. What then happens is the more the pursuer tries to force the distancer to stay, the more shut down the distancer becomes, and the more shut down the distancer becomes, the more anxious and assertive the pursuer becomes. You can see how this cycle is a recipe for disaster, and unfortunately, it is a common dynamic amongst many couples. To make matters more problematic, I have found for some reason pursuers and distancers are attracted to each other! Maybe it's because two pursuers would drive each other crazy, and two distancers would eventually stop talking all together. Either way, it is challenging—but it does present the opportunity to get good at owning your own emotions and learning to self-sooth.

In the instances when a distancer is forced to stay, my distancer clients have reported not being able to think straight. They also report feeling overwhelmed, and the longer they are "forced" to stay, the more suffocated they feel. What they are, of course, describing is being in the lower brain, where they lose access to higher brain thinking; this is why they can't think straight. The sense of suffocation if they stay in the dynamic speaks to the autonomic nervous system kicking fight, flight, or freeze into full gear and propelling the distancer into flee mode. So, for this person, a time-out is exactly what they need and want—no problem there.

But, for their counterpart, we have the opposite experience. The pursuer reports feeling extreme frustration, anxiety, and even panic if they cannot resolve the conflict before parting. These individuals have a difficult time with taking a time-out and will do everything they can to keep their partner from leaving. Many also report feeling like they do have access to higher brain thought processes, and interestingly, I have found this to be true with three exceptions: 1. They lack the ability to empathize, 2. They are focused solely on winning the argument, and 3. They are coming from a sense of urgency and panic and think the resolution of the conflict will make it better. Because of the symptoms above, we know they are in their lower brain. After all, their partner's needs, as well as the needs of the relationship, are no longer important and it becomes them against their partner. When we are activated, again it is kill or be killed, and we just want to gain the upper hand, which will hardly benefit the relationship. Also, the sense of urgency and panic is out of proportion to the situation, since nobody is in danger. Remember, if it feels urgent and nobody is bleeding or physically threatened, that is a tip-off that we are in the RB. Given all these internal qualities the pursuer is experiencing, we can safely say they are in the RB as well, so their access to logic and problem solving may seem available, but it is compromised. Knowing this, we arrive again at the conclusion that a conversation will not benefit either party when they are unable to access all their higher brain faculties. Even though the pursuer reacts to their triggers differently (likely being more of a fighter) than the distancer, they both need to get into their higher brain, so a time-out is necessary. Distancers would likely be fine to never deal with conflict at all, but that isn't healthy either. So, what will be most important with this intervention is to make the time-out temporary, with an end time—this is what makes it a compromise and hopefully more doable for the pursuer.

To institute a time-out effectively, I have had my couples in session, ahead of time, agree to a set time to come back with each other thereby applying structure and an end point to the time-out. This serves the added effect of quelling or lessening the pursuers fears around loss and rejection, just by knowing that there will be an end time to their separating and that it's not forever. In terms of who is declaring the time-out and end time in the moment during a conflict because pursuers have a harder time parting, I usually assign this to my distancers. They can say something like, "We need to take a time-out. Let's come back in an hour (or whatever time was agreed upon in session previously) and see if we are cooled off yet to resume this conversation. Are you okay with this?" By them checking in with their partner there is a sense of respect being communicated and partnership and hopefully the pursuer will be ok with the previously agreed upon end time. If they aren't, I still recommend parting. You don't want to end up arguing about the amount of time you are taking off and you don't want to remain engaged! And in order to establish trust with this technique it will be important to follow through with the end time and come back to discuss what happened. But once you do if either or both of you are still triggered you will have to again institute another time-out. Again, we are only ready to talk when we are in higher brain. And we don't implement time-outs to avoid conflict; we just postpone the conversation until we are in our right minds to have it.

You may even decide to make your time-out shorter than was previously agreed upon, sometimes all it takes is ten minutes to cool down, but other times, it may take longer or several time-outs. Also, I'm going against and age-old adage with this, but if your argument happens before bed—please, please, please go to bed angry! Take your break until the morning. Do not wait for hours and then try to talk it out as the clock is ticking toward dawn—that will likely lead to a massive amount of emotional escalation for one or both partners. There is nothing to be discussed when we are trigged *and* tired. Almost always after a good night's rest, we think more clearly. My husband and I used to have some heated arguments before bed, but once we learned to take a time-out until the morning, we found over and over again when we woke up, we couldn't even remember why we were arguing. Sleep has a way of getting you out of your RB.

What is important to remember is that for both the pursuer and the distancer, the anxiety they feel when in conflict is likely rooted in their past. This is again why unplugging from the relationship is crucial, we must do this in order to examine whether our triggers are rooted in the now or way back when. Ultimately, the time-out is necessary to aid us in figuring out what we are really feeling and why we are feeling it and quite simply, if we stay engaged in the relationship, we won't do this.

We can see that the pursuer has an underlying fear of abandonment or loss, which likely is historic, so it will be vital for the pursuer to explore where this comes from and to heal the original wound. Likewise, the distancer's response of fleeing may be rooted in past relationships as well, where they experienced a sense of engulfment, so now when they feel a conflict coming or a boundary violation, it sends them into an emotional tailspin. Because of the tendency for past scars to be at the root of extreme reactions for both parties, it will be important for both to heal whatever may be at the base of their need to pursue or distance respectively. And the reality also exists for both that it might be a personality style that the couple will need to work through, thereby finding ways to honor each other's process while also caring for the relationship.

After you take a time-out and implement self-care strategies, when you come back to your partner, you might not even need to work anything out. Once you are in the higher brain, you see things differently, so whatever it was that was bothering you might just fade away. Now, some people think if you don't work through the argument, then you are just sweeping it under the rug, but the reality is, if it doesn't bother you when you are in higher brain, then it's likely not really a huge issue within the relationship, especially because we tend to nitpick when we are in our lower brain, too.

Now, once you are in the HB, you might realize that it was truly a trigger activating past scars, and if this is the case, then it really had nothing to do with your current relationship. Again, most of the time, it is 95% past and 5% right now. With such a higher percentage rooted in past traumas, it's important to unplug from the relationship so you can heal the repressed emotions associated with another time. This will also help you detangle future triggers from your current situation. In fact, if you really work on your triggers as they arise, over time, you will get so familiar with them that you will know where they are rooted and if it truly is about something happening in your current relationship.

> *"Avoiding your triggers isn't healing. Healing*
> *happens when you're triggered and you're able to*
> *move through the pain, the pattern, and the story,*
> *and walk your way to a different ending."*
> — Vienna Pharaon

One of the most significant traumas I have experienced in my life was the death of my high school sweetheart. This was the trauma from when I was seventeen and this experience became an intense trigger later in life for me, it would rear its head repeatedly. I began working on healing the scar tissue from this loss before I met my husband which was almost 15 years after the incident itself. After several tumultuous relationships and a lot of heartbreak, in my early 30's, my psyche was finally ready to begin processing this trauma. So, when I met my husband at age 35, I felt this wound was significantly healed at least in comparison to where my healing was before. But predictably, the relationship, and more importantly my vulnerability in the relationship with my husband (then boyfriend), brought more of it to the surface.

Ultimately a set of circumstances would present themselves, and I would feel incredibly fearful, uneasy, and panicked. These feelings quickly led to wanting to break up and run from the relationship. Luckily, I knew this trigger pretty darn well, and I knew the impulse to run was my RB response to this trigger. What I ended up learning to do was when this trigger was activated, I would remove myself from interacting with my husband (my then boyfriend) as best I could. At first, this was difficult because he is more of a pursuer (of course!), but after a while, we learned to take time-outs, which really gave me the space I desperately needed. I came to learn that it was less about us and more about my scar tissue.

Once on a time-out, I would write in my journal to get to the root of it. The hard part was that my RB tried to convince me that the feelings I was having were tied to my current partner, so I would write a letter to him (without sending it) to get out whatever feelings were there. Sure enough, once I started writing, I got to the core of it—my past trauma. But before I arrived at this clarity it took a few years of some major arguments with my husband, which always resulted in a deeper exploration of the essence of

96

the argument and then a subsequent breakdown and breakthrough healing sessions on my own to start to lighten the load of repressed emotions tied to my past trauma. Over time I even stopped projecting any of this emotion onto my husband and owned that it was my past. In fact, I wouldn't even share it with my husband after a while. I knew it was something I had to work through on my own. And after many 'crying-my-eyes-out moments', what I started to notice was this trigger that was once a ten on the Richter scale (ten being the highest) soon became maybe a three.

Now, after a decade of those massive healing years, it's just about non-existent. The grief is still there (I don't think grief ever really goes away) but the trigger is gone. How cool is that? And if it wasn't for this relationship, which made me open to experiencing true vulnerability with another person, I likely wouldn't have been able to access a large portion of that repressed energy. This is where relationships really do have the power to heal as they attract any wound inside of us that has been buried out of necessity and bring it to the surface so we can heal it once and for all. And again, this healing is vital so we can remove the repressed energy inside of us, which will truly enable us to be intimate with another. Like bricks in a wall, our repressed emotions will block our ability for true connection with another person. The more we heal, the more connected we are to ourselves, the more connected, the more whole we are; the more whole the more authentic we become, and the more we can open up our hearts to another.

"Nobody is sent to anyone by accident."
— A Course in Miracles

Exercises

Let's pause for a moment and have you get clear which kind of partner you are (the pursuer or the distancer), how this manifests in your relationship, and ways you can manage this in terms of the coping skills you can use to self-sooth. Then let's explore your triggers in general.

Which type are you: _____

Self-soothing activities I can do when activated:

1. _____
2. _____
3. _____
4. _____
5. _____

Write down some ways to frame needing a time-out if you are a distancer (remember to add an end time) or self-talk strategies to help yourself manage the separation if you are a pursuer (i.e., what can you tell yourself to make it easier):

1. _____
2. _____
3. _____
4. _____

Now, let's have you explore a bit of your current triggers and how they tie back to the past. List below current triggers and the original cause of them:

1. Trigger (list what scenario activates it):

_____

_____

_____

What do you want to do in response to it (fight, flight, or freeze)?

_____

_____

_____

What original trauma or difficult event is it tied to?

_____

_____

_____

2. Trigger (list what scenario activates it):

_____

_____

_____

What do you want to do in response to it (fight, flight, or freeze)?

_____

_____

_____

What original trauma or difficult event is it tied to?

_____

_____

_____

3. Trigger (list what scenario activates it):

_____

_____

_____

What do you want to do in response to it (fight, flight, or freeze)?

_____

_____

_____

What original trauma or difficult event is it tied to?

_____

_____

_____

CHAPTER 6
Boundaries

What are healthy boundaries in relationships?

This chapter is a little bit of an extension of the last chapter, yet distinct enough to demand and require its own space. I remember in grad school, one of my professors was discussing the separation-individuation phase in childhood development, which is around two to three years. This is the stage in which we, as humans, realize we are separate from our caretakers, and we must learn how to embody our autonomy while connecting with others. This transition is fundamental to our development, and how we navigate this will be echoed later in life. If we are unable to navigate this phase in development successfully, we will have difficulties balancing our inner world with the outer world. In fact, the most severe personality disorders result from difficulties with this developmental stage, but the reality is this balancing act is something I think every human struggles with.

We are all tasked with the almost impossible dichotomy of staying connected to ourselves while at the same time connecting with others. When we achieve this balance, we have healthy attachment to others as well as a healthy relationship with ourselves. When first introduced to the topic of healthy boundaries, I remember thinking how unbelievably challenging this is for any human, and I think for most of us, we fall out of balance quickly and frequently. In fact, I bet most of you will say that you are either good at connecting with yourself or you are good at connecting with others, and likely not many will say they are good at doing both. We could also speak in terms of introversion and extroversion here, too. Introverts will likely be better at holding a connection to themselves versus another, whereas extroverts will likely be better at connecting with others despite themselves. In fact, the very definition spells this out: introverts' recharge by themselves, and extroverts' recharge by being with others. Both have arguments for why their way of being is "better" than the other, but the fact remains—we all need to connect with others, and we all need to connect to ourselves. If we don't, there will be imbalances and therefore "negative" consequences for either side.

Let's look a little more closely at how this shows up in a discussion about boundaries.

Dr. Murray Bowen, the father of family systems theory, talked about how our boundaries with others reflect our intrapersonal organization or emotional development. Bowen really zoned in on our ability to differentiate our thoughts from our feelings, and the more aware we are of our felt experience versus our cognitive experience, the more differentiated we are. This is when we know what we are thinking and what we are feeling, and the two don't get enmeshed or confused—which is a pretty hard task. Most people don't know what they are feeling, and some don't even know what they are thinking at a given moment. Therefore, the more self-aware you become, the better you get at being in tune to the different experiences going on inside of you. Once in tune, you soon get good at knowing what you are feeling versus knowing what you are thinking thereby becoming more emotionally healthy.

This really echoes the chapters on the reptilian brain, as well as repressed emotions. In order to navigate the activation of the lower brain, we have to get really good at knowing we are there, and the best way to know we are there is by looking at the quality of our thoughts, as well as our feelings. Increased self-awareness is the way toward being able to achieve all of this. Likewise, the goal in Bowen's mind for human development is differentiation of self internally, because the more differentiated we are, the more self-aware and organized we are and, therefore, the more emotionally evolved we are. This makes sense because if we know what we are thinking and we know what we are feeling, we are more equipped to learn how to manage both.

Going back to the reptilian brain, we also would get pretty good at not getting sucked into negative thoughts because we would catch them, making it easier to stay in the higher brain or, at least make our way back there. And likewise with our emotions, if we know what we are feeling, we will know what we need to do to help the emotional energy move so it doesn't get stuck. With increased awareness, we will naturally be moved to heal our repressed emotional energy resulting in wholeness and a greater clarity for what we feel and who we are in relation to those around us.

With Bowen's systems theory, it is further theorized that how differenti-ated we are internally will reflect how differentiated we are externally in our relationships with others, and the more differentiated we are with others, the healthier our boundaries will be in general. This again makes sense, because if we are good at knowing what we are thinking and we are good at knowing how we are feeling, we are going to be good at knowing how to relate to others in a way that honors what is healthy for us. We won't violate our boundaries because that wouldn't feel good, and if we are in tune with our inner world, we will be motivated to respond and behave in a way that honors our integrity. Bowen expands on this more in depth with the three most common types of boundaries: *enmeshed, rigid,* and *flexible.*

Enmeshed boundaries

Enmeshed boundaries are when the boundary we have between ourselves and others is highly porous, to the point of being nonexistent. Enmeshment is when we get lost within another person; we join the other so compre-hensibly that we no longer experience a separate sense of self. This type of boundary also reflects an internal enmeshment between thoughts and feelings, as this individual doesn't experience or isn't aware of the differ-ence between their felt experience versus their cognitive experience.

Relationships with this individual will likely be codependent because their identity will be rooted in the relationship with the other. With this boundary, we have an abandonment of connection with self in favor of connection with other. A type of an enmeshed boundary is a "pleaser"— this is when one becomes reluctant or even fearful to speak their truth because it might compromise the longevity of the relationship. They hold back anything that might cause conflict to avoid confrontation, discom-fort, or displeasing the other. The problem with this, of course, is that once an individual stops speaking their truth, they stop knowing what their truth is, and then they come to lose touch with themselves. When this happens, they no longer are aware of what they are thinking or feeling so they lose the differentiation between thoughts and feelings. Becoming totally enmeshed in their relationship, "they" are no longer there—there is no "I" only "us"—hence there is also a lack of differentiation between self and other. As Bowen predicted, our internal organization will always reflect our boundaries with others. If we are not differentiated internally, we will not be differentiated externally.

A pleaser, at times, can be the rock or the emotional caretaker in the relationship, too. This is where they do everything for the other person, and their self-sacrifice brings a sense of nobility and self-lessness. Like was mentioned in the chapter on emotions- traditional females fall into this role often. I've worked with numerous pleasers that gratuitously give, and initially, this is something they derive a lot of esteem from. But this is actually damaging to not only themselves (which they don't mind, of course, as the self-sacrifice is what feels good), but also to their partner and I'll describe to you why that is through what I call the "backpack analogy."

This is the deal—we are all born with a backpack. In fact, the goal in life is to get good at carrying our backpack. In our backpack is everything that is ours to carry: our past scars, family dynamic, childhood issues, current emotional state, triggers, addictions and thought processes. When we carry our backpack enough, we get pretty darn good at knowing how to carry it. So, if, at any point, someone comes over and hands you their backpack or you decide because you love them so much and they seem to be struggling that you will heroically carry their backpack for them, you then have two issues to deal with.

The first issue, and the most obvious one, is you just doubled your weight in backpacks! How on earth can you carry both long term? Quite simply, you can't. Eventually, this will get to be too much, and you will start to feel overwhelmed and likely resentful of your partner (or family member or friend) for having to carry their load.

The second issue grabs people's attention right away and convinces them that maybe being a pleaser isn't such a noble thing is. That is, by carrying your partner's backpack, you just robbed them of getting good at carrying their backpack. After all, it is their job to learn how to do this. And when they learn to do this, they get good at it and feel pretty darn good about themselves because of their sense of self-sufficiency, and they know they can make it through life carrying their backpack. When you take their backpack, you take this away from them. Moreover, they will soon become totally reliant on you to carry their backpack all the time, so what happens when you are sick or on a trip without them or maybe even pass away? What will they do? They will become convinced they never could carry their backpack, and on some level, they are deficient and their self-esteem plummets. Knowing we can carry our backpack no matter what challenges life brings provides a sense of stability in oneself and self-reliance. We know we can handle things because we've handled them our whole life. It also gives us something to do and focus on, without which could lead to unhealthy habits and addictions. It has been noted that one of the main reasons why people use substances is boredom. As St. Jerome said, *"Idle hands is the devil's workshop"*.

This all blaringly highlights the problem with codependency and enmeshment: it harms both individuals, and it also it harms the relationship itself. If there is no "I" in the relationship, you aren't really experiencing intimacy, so it also robs the relationship of true connection.

Intimacy comes when we open ourselves to another and share our experiences and our truth. If you aren't a separate person, there is no "you" and therefore no "your truth" to share. Going back to not knowing what you think or feel, many times when you are enmeshed, if you lose touch with yourself, you simply won't know yourself enough to share yourself with someone else. Further, codependency and enmeshed boundaries will also lead to acting-out behaviors because of the discomfort that comes from having your sense of self outside of you. If you NEED the other person to feel safe, you will naturally be terrified to lose this connection.

With many clients, I've seen extreme forms of jealously and intense exertions of control over each other. Emotional escalation and triggers manifest more in enmeshed relationships. When put in the context of a lack of differentiation between thoughts and feelings, this makes sense because the individual triggered will have a hell of a time knowing what they are feeling or thinking, and they likely won't be able to discern if their partner is responsible or if it's past scars. Because there is more of a focus on the other and the relationship and not a focus on oneself, the lack of boundaries automatically dissolves opportunities for self-reflection. With enmeshed boundaries the individual is always focused outside themselves and on the other person. They will likely use the phrase, "You made me feel . . ." a lot and will naturally have difficulties taking a time-out and owning their own emotional reactions. When there is no demarcation between self and other, there is no clarity—and, again, with a lack of demarcation between thoughts and feelings internally, they won't know what their experience is and/or who/what is influencing or causing it.

Due to their fixation on their partner and the relationship, they will also likely try to change their partner or control their partner's behaviors. I had one instructor in college say that codependency follows the illogical thought that says, "I need you to change in order for me to feel better." In this way, the codependent partner is focused outside of themselves always to feel better. From this stance, they will naturally become highly agitated and escalated if they cannot connect or the connection feels lost or compromised, and they will seek to retore it at all costs. This is also why I see codependency to be a form of an addiction, where you need to merge with the other to feel safe in the world and are always chasing the original high of connection that you experienced when you first met and the fantasy that this connection with someone will complete you and heal all your original wounds. But the utopian relationship you chase after will always elude you because you are now too enmeshed to experience anything subjectively.

Individuals in enmeshed/codependent relationships also have a very challenging time if and when the relationship ends. It will feel like a part of them died, and they will feel lost until they finally rebuild the lost connection with themselves. Many clients have come into session to discover that they have no idea how to soothe or what coping activities work for them. This is because they were so focused on having their cup filled by others that they have completely forgotten how to fill it themselves. A lot of times it's also because they were in an enmeshed relationship with a caretaker, so they never learned how to fill their cup to begin with. Ultimately for this attachment style, it will be vital for them to learn how to go inward and to begin to discover who they really are. Once they can learn how to self-soothe, they can begin to explore their thoughts and feelings, thereby putting them on a trajectory of emotional health, increased self-awareness, balance, and wholeness.

> *"Daring to set boundaries is about having the courage to love ourselves even when we risk disappointing others."*
> — Brené Brown

Rigid boundaries

Rigid boundaries are another way we show up in relationships. This boundary indicates a highly delineated way of being with others. This is when the individual doesn't join at all with other people and is emotionally distant. In this way, the individual is detached in their relationships with others and more focused on remaining isolated within themselves. What makes this type of boundary unhealthy is the fact that there is not only a disconnect between self and other, but there is also a disconnect between thinking and feeling, with thinking likely being the only valid aspect of this individual's experience. This individual lives life from their minds and their feelings are completely segregated to their unconscious. When asked how they are feeling, someone with rigid boundaries will likely respond with a thought. For example, one of my clients when asked how they feel stated: "I feel that so and so needs to work on dealing with their anger better". Or another client's response: "I feel that we need to implement more communication techniques". These answers obviously don't contain anything resembling a feeling and yet for both clients it was a valid response to the question.

It's interesting how this way of being reflects a disconnection from both self and other, because I think in a lot of ways, we learn how we feel by expressing ourselves to another. Going back to the nature of emotions, the way we process repressed emotions and the way we stay connected to our emotional landscape is through verbalizing our feelings to the world, thereby experiencing validation and a sense of emotional understanding.

If you are cut off from others, you naturally won't engage in and experience the completion of any of your emotional loops, not unless you are really doing some deep individual work and likely with a therapist. But even if you did engage in treatment to access your emotions, what then would happen is a connection between thoughts and feelings and inevitably the discovery of the need to connect with others. Again, we find that the outer–inner boundary is indeed a mirror of each other.

Because they are lacking access to their emotional life, those that are used to this type of boundary will naturally lack the empathy needed to really connect and be intimate with another. Because our emotions connect us to others, this individual will also naturally have difficulties seeing other viewpoints, as well as maintaining healthy long-term relationships. However, it could be said that this type of boundary has more mature and evolved defense mechanisms because they live life from their minds. However, at the end of the day, what this really translates to is being good at emotional compartmentalization and repression.

What do flexible/healthy boundaries look like?

Now, we will move toward what healthy boundaries look like. Healthy boundaries are when we have a good sense of separation between self and other: we can connect to others while remaining connected to ourselves, and we can spend time with others but know that we also need to fill our own cup (i.e., spend time with ourselves doing our daily practices and coping mechanisms, etc.). From practicing healthy boundaries, because they are so balanced externally, this individual will also have a healthy organization of self internally; they are aware of their thoughts and can differentiate them with their feelings. They will also be flexible in how they connect with others and how they connect with themselves. Because there is a sense of stability inside themselves, there is also no need to be rigid and no need to be anxiously attached to others through enmeshment. This individual is grounded inside themselves and so they can maintain a healthy outer/inner boundary.

*"Walls keep everybody out. Boundaries teach people
where the door is."*
— Mark Groves

With healthy boundaries, of course, the challenge is to maintain them. Every day is different—that is, just when you hit a good balance and have healthy boundaries one day, the next day, you might fall back into enmeshed or rigid boundary patterns or tendencies. But knowing what you can do to maintain a healthy balance is something you can learn, and as you heal and learn to stay in your higher brain, you will be more equipped to consistently differentiate thoughts from feelings, as well as self from other.

I have broken down a few different strategies to support you in doing this:

- Make sure to set aside time to do your daily practices (mind/emotions, body, and spirit).
- Speak your truth (authenticity is vital in maintaining your sense of self).
- Own what is yours and what isn't; do not take on someone else's backpack.
- Make sure you are not on the constant go and that you have built in down time to just be. In modern day society, we are so go, go, go, we become human 'doings' and we forget to be human beings. There are times that we need to just stop and breathe. Our daily practices help us to do this, but if you are constantly plugging into others, you might start to feel a bit unstable or out of control. Those feelings are a good indicator that you are likely focused outside of yourself too much.
- Make sure to also have enough social time on the calendar. If we have rigid boundaries, we likely isolate ourselves too much from the world, and this will likely lead to disconnection and loneliness.

Exercises

Let's now explore which boundary you identify with or which you might have tendencies toward and how that shows up in your relationships:

Type of boundary you have tendencies toward: _____

Behaviors that tell you that you are living life from this boundary:

_____

_____

_____

_____

_____

_____

What do you need to be doing in your daily life to ensure you are not falling back into your pattern? For example, if you have enmeshed tendencies, make sure you are doing your daily practices, not taking on other people stuff, and speaking your truth. If you have rigid boundaries, maybe you need to focus more on expressing your emotions, exploring your emotions through journaling or verbalizing feelings to others, and having social outings planned on the calendar, etc.

_____

_____

_____

_____

_____

_____

CHAPTER 7
Moving Forward—Goal Setting

Now that we have gone through and discussed the different elements that will enhance your ability to heal and live your truth; staying out of the reptilian brain, healing repressed emotions, amplifying, and strengthening positive self-talk, exploring and healing triggers in relationships, and navigating the incredibly challenging balancing act of connecting to others and yourself at the same time, let's talk about next steps.

How do you want to incorporate this information moving forward? What is your take-away for now?

We have covered a lot of ground, so it's okay if you haven't had the chance to delve into each area. If that is the case, perhaps you would like to keep your focus narrow. Or maybe, instead, you would like to work toward incorporating all the different facets that can lead you to becoming a whole, healed, and authentic human being. Either way, this chapter on goal setting will help you transition and integrate all this information into your daily life (and skip any questions that don't apply).

> *"Setting goals is the first step in turning the invisible into the visible."*
> — Tony Robbins

Exercises

Let's start chapter by chapter in terms of the commitment you would like to make starting with your daily practices:

1. You hopefully have identified your "just three things." What are the three activities you need to be doing daily for your mind/emotion, body, and spirit (remember you can have more than one for each category and fluctuate) that will keep you in your higher brain?

Mind/Emotions:_____

Body:_____

Spirit:_____

2. What are the strategies that work best in helping you to manage your triggers when they happen, thereby getting you up in your higher brain?

_____

_____

_____

_____

_____

_____

_____

3. What are some ways you can ensure you are processing and/or soothing your emotions as they arise (e.g., talking to others, journaling, listening to music or a certain song, etc.)?

_____

_____

_____

_____

_____

_____

_____

4. What are the traumas that would be good for you to continue to process and heal (rank them in order to intensity)?

a. _____
b. _____
c. _____
d. _____
e. _____
f. _____
g. _____
h. _____
i. _____
j. _____

5. What are some automatic thoughts or beliefs that you would like to continue to work on, correct and heal?

a. _____
b. _____
c. _____
d. _____
e. _____
f. _____

6. What are some thoughts that come straight from your higher brain (i.e., the angel on your shoulder) in response to the ACBs or thoughts above?

a. _____
b. _____
c. _____
d. _____
e. _____
f. _____

7. What are some strategies you can use when in conflict with your partner (this could also be family members or anyone else in your life)?

a. _____
b. _____

    c. _____

    d. _____

    e. _____

    f. _____

8. Name three strategies you can implement to build healthier, flexible boundaries with others in your life, where you can connect with another while also remaining connected to yourself?

    a. _____

    b. _____

    c. _____

CONCLUSION

My intention in writing this book is to help you create your own owner's manual for how to navigate your internal processes, as well as how to navigate processing all the things that have been, and will be, thrust upon you in this life. It's *your* owner's manual because what works for each person will be unique to that individual and the work is about discovering what works for YOU.

The good news is as idiosyncratic as the work is, I've discovered after working with clients for a couple of decades that the therapeutic process does center around two fundamental activities:

- building skill sets (coping skills, communication skills, conflict resolution skills, effective communication, boundary setting, etc.); and
- healing what needs to heal.

My hope is the journey through this book gives you a whole lot of both! With the development of your "just three things" and strategies to interrupt lower-brain activation, as well as lower-brain self-talk, you will start to feel better. Neuroscience has proven that when we are doing activities that are healthy for us, i.e., higher-brain activities, our brain is bathed in all those feel-good neurotransmitters. So, what you will learn quickly is that it works! And the feel-good feelings will become so reinforcing that you will automatically go for those activities again. Your practices will start to become second nature because you are also establishing and strengthening new neural pathways that make the higher-brain activity choice a more readily available resource.

Just keep reminding yourself that quite simply what you do every day, and every moment, matters more than anything else. So, if you happen to feel lousy right now, stop what you are doing and immediately go back to your higher-brain activity list. Remind yourself that lousy feelings that are likely tied to lousy thoughts are all an illusion—and remember those lousy feelings are messengers telling you to do something different! So, take heed and change your course in that moment. You are literally one higher brain activity away from feeling significantly better!

As you are implementing those higher-brain strategies, which hopefully help you to feel better sooner than later, also remember that healing what needs to heal is just as vital in breaking up the figurative scar tissue that binds the reptilian brain to the amygdala. It is our scars that keep us imprisoned to our lower brain, destined to experience mental health symptoms, and it is through healing our scars that we can be set free from our anxiety, depression, addictions, triggers and so on, so we can truly choose how we want to experience life. Without processing the repressed emotional responses from our past, we will always be drawn back to our lower-brain processes and symptoms. And healing what needs to heal also holds the most potential to link you to a deeper part of yourself, accessing a sense of wholeness. The goal again is not perfection or happiness, but authenticity and wholeness. The more you heal, the more you release repressed energies, the more connected you become to yourself and the more 'you', you become. More 'you' is truly the goal. It was once said that there is no one like you—that is your superpower. Or as Rachel Ramen put it, "Healing may not be so much about getting better, as about letting go of everything that isn't you—all of the expectations, all of the beliefs—and becoming who you are."

Once you have found a deeper connection with yourself and your truth, you will be able to achieve healthy relationship interactions and you will be better equipped to manage your triggers and heal emotional material when it surfaces. Our relationships reflect where we are in our development, so as you become healthier on the inside, your world on the outside becomes healthier too. This will inevitably lead you to having a balance with boundaries because you will know what is aligned with your truth and what isn't and, hopefully, you will also learn how to assert your boundaries when needed and lean on others when you need help too. The balance of self and other is the most challenging, so be gentle with yourself as you are figuring this all out.

We walk this journey called life not to live happily ever after but to learn how to walk authentically, no matter what is thrown at us, and to allow whatever our emotional truth is in the moment to be there unapologetically, raw, and real. Hopefully, the tools in this book arm you with the knowledge and self-awareness to support you in living your most authentic life, a life filled with real interactions and emotional truths.

And once you learn how to sit with your truth and how to embody where you have been and let it make you into the whole and authentic version of yourself, you will become a beacon for others who cross your path. Once we find our own liberation, we become a shining light for others so they can learn to do the same. While the hardest battles teach us the most, it's also the recovery from those battles that makes us the most equipped to help others. Once we walk the terrain, we are uniquely endowed with the ability to support others in doing the same. Our trauma enables us to help others through their pain because we know it so well, and by helping others we get to the next level of our own healing. In this way, our pain becomes transmuted into something profoundly beautiful; the moment we realize we can help others because of what we have been through our suffering is no longer in vain.

"Sometimes to overcome your darkness, you must
become the light for someone else."
— Author Unknown

May you continue to discover more and more pieces of yourself, because as you do, you will inevitably stumble upon the magic that is inside you. Inside of all of us is a Light that connects us to each other, and when we go within, we stumble upon the profound truism that we are never alone and through our actualized wholeness and authenticity we can embody and emulate our truth, which enables us to illuminate more light to the world.

ABOUT THE AUTHOR

Aimee Semas-Day, LMFT has a master's in clinical psychology with a holistic emphasis. She is a licensed marriage and family therapist and has a thriving private practice in California. She has worked with individuals in a therapeutic setting for the past two decades and has successfully implemented her unique treatment modality in working with a variety of diagnosis and mental health symptoms. Aimee, herself, experienced numerous traumas growing up and suffered from depression for over fifteen years. Because of this experience, Aimee was drawn to psychology as a way to navigate and understand her own pain and found a sense of meaning and purpose in helping others. Through her journey of seeking understanding, she gleaned insight into the human condition and while helping others heal, she was also able to process her own pain on a deeper, more complete level. Coupling her own therapeutic process with researching how the brain and psyche work, Aimee came to find the answers she was seeking, and by applying the concepts in this book to herself, Aimee has been depression free for over a decade. Because of the positive results that came from specific healing techniques she experienced in her own healing as well as the observed successes these techniques have had in her clinical work, Aimee was compelled to write and share this information with the world. The concept and strategies in *Heal* can truly evoke deeper healing and a greater ability for authenticity and wholeness. Aimee has also written *Heroes and Butterflies: Breaking Relationship Patterns* (CreateSpace, 2009). Along with her master's in psychology, Aimee is a credentialed CMT, NLP life coach and yoga instructor. She lives in Morgan Hill, California, with her husband, daughter, stepson, and two Shih Tzu puppies.

To get a multimedia experience of the concepts in this book, check out Aimee's YouTube channel at:

https://www.youtube.com/channel/UC5RKhBG-EZ4o5OkxbLlKHRA